FINGERS
IN THE
Frosting

GOD'S HAND ON THE CREATION OF OH MY CUPCAKES!

MELISSA M. JOHNSON

Printed in the United States of America.
Book design by Lauren E. Halgerson.

Melissa J. Creative
5015 S. Western Avenue, Suite 290
Sioux Falls, SD 57108
melissajcreative.com

To Randi, Emily and Brandon ... in all of my lifetime, my greatest legacy is you.

INDEX

Introduction 7

Dream a ~~Little~~ Big Dream 11

1. Know Your Values 21

2. Know Your Vision. 37

3. Know Your Purpose 49

4. Know Your Worth. 61

5. Know Your Product 73

6. Know Your Audience 81

7. Know Your Strengths 93

8. Know Your Boundaries. 111

9. Know Your Win 123

10. Know Your Self 131

11. Know Your God 143

A BRIEF HISTORY OF
OH MY CUPCAKES!

Melissa is working in radio when she reads a story about cupcake shops and their popularity across the nation. First intrigued, she becomes obsessed and starts learning everything she can about cupcakeries.

The cupcake obsession continues to grow with Melissa visiting as many cupcakeries as she can find, while still working in radio.

May
Melissa leaves radio for a job which turns out not to be the path she would eventually end up following. Cupcakes, full steam ahead!

June
Fictitious business name is registered with the state of South Dakota as "Cupcake Days". Graphic design goddess Lauren starts working on logos and has entire Cupcake Days logo created.

July

Fictitious business name is re-registered with the state of South Dakota as Oh My Cupcakes! after Brandon (age 5 at the time) starts using the exclamation in conversation and Melissa thinks, "Oh for cute. Wouldn't that be a great business name?" Graphic design goddess Lauren says, "No big!" and re-designs logo to reflect new business name.

August

Melissa develops business plan after falling in love with a space in The Bridges at 57th and Western. Business plan in hand, walks confidently into bank and talks to really nice banker named Ryan. Boldly asks for $40,000. Ryan doesn't exactly say no, but doesn't exactly say yes. Best "not exactly yes" in history of mankind.

August

Commercial kitchen space between bowling alley and liquor store is subleased from a generous and kind man named Dan.

August 21

Oh My Cupcakes has first "official" order and first official day in business.

September

Brianna hops aboard Team Cupcake Ninja.

2010

February 14

Oh My Cupcakes! celebrates our first Valentine's Day with a fundraiser called the "Randy Special" for Randy Weber who had been paralyzed in a car accident. Overwhelmed with orders. Call in favors from every friend and family member we know as we work through the night to keep up. Write a check to the family for $1,200 from proceeds of orders. Humbled and amazed at what God can do with cupcakes.

April 1
Grand Opening day in our new digs, our downtown store at 524 N. Main Avenue. Still just Brianna and me, we add intern Mary Kate and part timer Ashley, (cue the jokes) along with a few other fill in characters. Early days in the store give new meaning to "getting by with a little help from my friends."

· 2011 ·

Expansion and growth happens so quickly, everyone hangs on for the ride. Some mistakes. Many learning opportunities.

March
Nationwide shipping begins. Cupcakes ship to many states and to recipients at Amazon, the New York Yankees and The Jon Gordon Companies.

· 2012 ·

Oh My Cupcakes! grows from Melissa and Brianna and a couple of part timers to a full-fledged operation with about 17-20 Cupcake Ninjas.

August
Oh My Cupcakes! hits one million dollars in sales. What is life? This is craziness.

September
Amanda joins the Oh My Cupcakes! team, part time at first, and helps create new processes that take Oh My Cupcakes! to the next level.

November

OhMyCupcakes.com gets a major facelift and a user-friendly, functional shopping cart. Now you can order cupcakes online at 2 am in your footie jammies.

2013

April 25, 2013

Melissa signs agreement to lease space in The Bridges at 57th and Western. Designers to build a space exactly to our needs and specs.

April 25, 2013

Melissa wins Tribute to Women award in Executive Leadership category. Super humbled and excited. Surrounded by Cupcake Ninjas, family and love.

May 2013

Oh My Cupcakes! named Woman Owned Business of the Year for the whole stinkin' State of South Dakota. Ridiculously honored, dumbfounded.

Summer 2013

Work through design and finishes for dream space at Bridges at 57th and Western. So much fun to see dream fully come together. Paint colors, cabinetry and design workflow . . . watching the dream develop is surreal.

August 6, 2013

Move into and open gorgeous and spacious new storefront in The Bridges at 57th and Western.

The move to the Bridges brings next level of growth. Team of Cupcake Ninjas grows to 30.

July
Oh My Cupcakes! adds employer-matched retirement benefits.

August
Celebrate 5 year anniversary with party hats, limited edition cupcakes and special events.

October
Health insurance is added for employees, with Oh My Cupcakes! paying a part of the premium cost.

October 15
Oh My Cupcakes! opens second location, a cupcake kiosk in the Empire Mall.

2015

June
Nearly 2 years after the move from downtown into the Bridges location, the Oh My Cupcakes! corporate offices are nearly organized. Reality, folks.

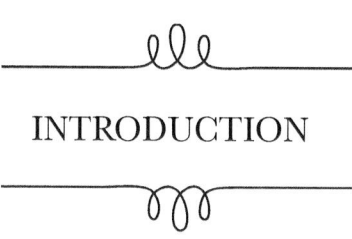

INTRODUCTION

Before you read one sentence in this book, I need to make a tiny confession. Come in close, lean in so you can hear me: I don't *really* know what I'm doing. If you're sad because you just spent your hard earned dollars on a book about how to grow your dreams . . . and the first thing I admit is I don't know exactly how it's done?

Sorry about it. But it's true.

Or if you're standing in the aisle at the book store sipping a latte and browsing the pages of this book right now, debating whether or not you're going to spend your hard earned dollars on it, go ahead and put it down if you're looking for the bona fide expert who guarantees they have the answers and will tell you everything you need to know to certify success and build fortune. If success and fortune are what you're after . . . I'm not your girl and this is not your book.

I used to say I had *no* idea what I was doing and it's pretty much true. When I tell you about some of the stupid mistakes we made along the way, you'll laugh along with me, (just hopefully not altogether at my expense.) We've learned. We know more now than we knew then, and I've got *some* idea what I'm doing now because we've grown from those mistakes along this journey. But I sure didn't have a clue what I was doing six years ago when things began.

Though I've grown, I'm certainly no expert. I'm kind of an accidental business woman. I feel mostly uncomfortable in a suit jacket and I don't even own a pair of dress pants. I'm all words and cupcakes, glitter and creativity. If I'm going to be totally honest with you right out of the chute, I'll tell you that I still drive past the Oh My Cupcakes! sign on 57th street outside of our beautiful store in the upscale development where it resides, and I struggle to believe it's really mine. Can it be? Really? Can a sign up on that big brick and digital signpost be something I'm responsible for? Can that logo be something that originated (somewhat) from my brain and can the name of that big place really have come so many years ago from my young son's lips?

The truth is, there's no way I could be totally responsible for it. I didn't do this alone. I still struggle to believe we are where we are today, and I still struggle with feeling worthy of it all sometimes. But I know we did a lot of things right, so that's what you and I are going to talk about through these pages ahead.

Oh My Cupcakes! started with $67 and some healthy desperation, and somehow grew to a company now valued at over 2 million dollars. We are thirty Cupcake Ninjas strong, ship nationwide and sell our product in our store's two locations. You guys, as much as I'd like to take credit, I did not do this, God did. God, fervent prayer, and a lot of people along the way who encouraged me and worked very hard alongside of me.

I don't have all the answers, I certainly don't do everything right, and I'm sure there are a number of people who will line up to tell you all the things we have done wrong and continue to do wrong. What I can tell you is how we got from there to here. How I became an accidental leader. How it all started with $67 and a cupcake dream but how it's become about so much more.

I don't know what your passion is, but if you've got a dream in your heart, I can tell you I've stood right there and I know how it feels. Are you feeling a little uncertain? Does it feel uncomfortable and just . . . gray and looming and shapeless right now? Maybe you're a little scared to risk, afraid of stepping outside of what feels comfortable, and you're a little hesitant to even dare to dream to begin. It's ok. You might not even know what your dream is yet, not fully, but you know you're restless and built for more.

Stick with me, and we can work through some of these fears together. We're going to try to overcome them with the power of storytelling. (I love telling stories and listening to great stories, don't you?) We can work through some of your hesitations, hand in hand. If you don't yet have a specific dream but you know you want more, maybe we can work on figuring out what it is. If you know what your passion is but you're afraid to start, we'll talk about that too.

I can't promise your dream will come true in exactly the way you're dreaming it right now, nor that you'd even want it to . . . not really. As you'll learn, success doesn't always show up to the party dressed in the clothes you think it will be wearing; it doesn't always look just like you think it should.

What I can promise is if you work harder than you ever imagined, you will see rewards which are greater than you can even foresee right now.

We got here without debt, and I really believe you can, too. We got here without rich relatives, so don't let that hold you back if you don't have a loaded aunt or uncle or grandma hiding out somewhere. I sure didn't. I don't possess a college education but I'm intelligent and well-spoken and I know how to work hard and solve problems when they come up. I know how to smile authentically at people and to treat them with the respect and kindness I'd like in return. If you have those qualities, you can do this. Did you hear me? *You can do this!* Not *just* like we did, but in your own, uniquely beautiful and amazing way.

Listen, I'm the first one to tell you there's a whole lot I don't understand about how we got here. But I can tell you what I do know, and the eleven specific things I'll tell you are what's gotten Oh My Cupcakes! where it is today. Though I'm no expert, I'll tell you what I've learned so far and maybe it can help you, too.

Are you ready to reach? To stretch? To step slightly outside of that circle of comfort you've built around yourself? We'll walk hand in hand. Let's go.

Ephesians 3:20

Now all glory to God, who is able, through his mighty power at work within us, to accomplish infinitely more than we might ask or think.

DREAM A ~~LITTLE~~ BIG DREAM

I had an idea seven years ago. I wanted to have a gourmet cupcakery. I knew that I had to start somewhere, but I'd hear the words "startup business" and cringe. True, you have to earn your stripes when you're starting out, but I never wanted to be a *startup* business. I wanted to instantly be an established business, a gorgeous storefront cupcakery where people would come for birthdays, weddings, anniversaries and other special moments.

Startup business? I've never been the kind of girl who does anything small. I wanted to create a business whose legacy would sustain generations. I wanted to make an impact on our community, make a measurable difference in people's lives and put my kids through college. I wanted to encourage women to reach for their own dreams, see families make their house payments and buy groceries and have the flexibility to go to their kids' preschool Christmas programs.

But *startup* is exactly where we started. It's where everyone starts. It's how it was supposed to be, exactly as it should have been. Back then, I did not want anyone to visit our "gourmet cupcakery." There was no storefront, no beautiful bakery cases, no cupcake shop where people could walk in the door and experience all that I wanted them to experience by way of guest service and smiles.

Oh My Cupcakes! started with $67. We rented space month-to-month in a sketchy commercial kitchen space sandwiched smack dab between a bowling alley and a liquor store. Back then it was only some ovens and a back-alley entrance. You guys, this place didn't have heat. We got the residual heat from the two businesses we were snuggled between. To use the bathroom, we had to walk through the liquor store (where we made great friends with James behind the counter.) In the middle of winter, we would open the doors to the convection ovens to warm up the circulation in our freezing fingertips.

We were a "delivery only" company back then. We had a one-page informational website with a phone number (my cell phone) where you could place your order. Sometimes people would place an order and want to pick up their cupcakes. I'd be all service and smiles on the phone, "Oh no, it's fine! We'll bring them to you! It's no trouble at all! We deliver!" Sometimes people would call at 2 am and decide they needed cupcakes, and I'd be woken from my slumber to slurred words and people with an after-bar cupcake crisis.

On so many levels, the beginning wasn't pretty. There were no vintage chandeliers or fun dining room seating and it was pretty tough to visualize how I was going to reach all of those dreams at first.

Only my closest friends were allowed to see the reality, the beginning of Oh My Cupcakes! My friend Sue had an order one day and came to pick up her cupcakes and as she left out the back alley entrance, she said she was looking over her shoulder and felt like she had just "done a deal." Her words you guys, not mine. When I was dreaming of my beautiful cupcakery, this kitchen space was definitely not the place I had envisioned.

But you need to know this: that commercial kitchen was beautiful in its own way. It was our spectacular and amazing origin, our grand starting point. The trajectory of our path was forever altered by our beginning there. The kitchen was exactly what we needed at the time we needed it: certified by the Department of Health; it was official and legit. Back then it was just Brianna and I (you'll be introduced to Brianna in a bit, stick with me) and back then we only did cupcakes baked-to-order so there's no way I could have sustained the overhead of a full storefront location. I had big, grand dreams but I needed to start small. I didn't *want* to start small, but God knew just what we needed. Even if it's not necessarily what I would have chosen, God knew what was best.

I was blessed to find a kind man named Dan who graciously sub-leased the space to us and let us bake cupcakes in his rented space for that season. For all the joking around I may do about our humble beginnings and no heat and the bathroom in the liquor store, I never want to discount the fact that we were given an opportunity in being there, for which I'm eternally grateful. We were able to rent the space from month to month, and that was a gift.

Still . . . to connect the dots from commercial kitchen starting line to the realization of big dreams? Please! I could scarcely even SEE those dreams. But I had to start somewhere, and

Philippians 4:19

And this same God who takes care of me will supply all your needs from his glorious riches, which have been given to us in Christ Jesus.

Dream a
little
BIG
DREAM

I had to dream big. So I dreamt of the things I wanted to do *with* Oh My Cupcakes! once we had a storefront space. I concentrated on the things I wanted us to be about creating for our guests, like making people to feel happy when they walked in the door. I wanted people to put their cares aside for at least a few minutes so they could just sink into the warm and cozy feelings cupcakes bring.

I wanted people to linger for a while over a cupcake and a cup of coffee and build relationships. I dreamed of seeing little nose and hand prints all over the bakery cases because kiddos had pressed their faces and fingers against the glass in delight and anticipation. (Yes, yes, I know I didn't even have bakery cases yet, that's totally my point here.)

I was creating dreams bigger than commercial kitchens and subleased space. I was serving imaginary people in my imaginary storefront with a big smile on my face, and making little kids feel a specific feeling when they walked in . . . even though there wasn't an "in" to walk into just yet. Maybe that sounds goofy, but it worked for me. I couldn't yet connect the dots or see my way into my beautiful bakery storefront, but I was dreaming my way there just the same.

I love to drink coffee in the cozy chairs at the Starbucks right across the street from Oh My Cupcakes! Sally and Amanda, Mercedes and Justin know my drink without even asking: Venti toffee nut latte, nonfat, add whip. (And they always spell my name right. Heart.) Much of this book was written at that very Starbucks, and every afternoon that I'm the "writer in residence," Amanda has me close the shades when the sun starts to descend over the west side of the building, so the store doesn't get overwarm. I tease them that I should have a little gold nameplate over one of the tables with my name on it. Hasn't happened yet, but I'm waiting for the day. Just . . . waiting.

Many times, people (women in particular) will call me up and ask if we can have coffee and discuss their business idea. Hello! An opportunity to sit in the cozy chairs, drink a toffee nut latte and discuss dreams? Heck yes I can make time for that.

Not every discussion is the same of course, but so many times in conversations it becomes clear that people have trouble thinking beyond six months or so into their business planning. We always seem to think in the tasks of the now.

Gosh, in the beginning it all looks so large and looming it seems daring to dream so big. I was there at first, I get it. But I want to encourage you to do your best to dream bigger than startup business, forecast further than simple "here's my business idea" to "this is the impact it's going to have on the community." If you're loving what I'm saying right now and you're feeling, "Oh gosh, I really need to hear more about that," go ahead and skip ahead to the "Know Your Vision" section. You'll find more good stuff there that expands on this even further. Meanwhile, dream big with me for a moment:

Here's my business idea: _____

_____

Here's my *dream*: _____

_____

_____

_____

_____

I'd encourage you to put some details on that dream. Make it a big and far-reaching dream. What do you want to do *with* what you're doing, for instance? Do you want to pay off your mortgage in 5 years and travel to Europe? Do you want to donate money to buy a well in Africa so people can have fresh water to drink? What sort of an impact do you want to make on the world?

Don't dream a little dream. Dream a *big* dream. I know it's tough to look out beyond a few months because you're in the planning and executing and tasking and working stages. That doesn't change for a while, if ever. But do your best to look way off into the distance for a moment, gaze down the road not just six months but maybe six years . . . and ask yourself what you want when you arrive there.

It'll be here before you know it.

Let's start with what scares you. What are your fears? Name them here.

I gave you lots of lines and lots of room for your fears. But now let's do something different. Let's change the outcome of those fears by telling ourselves a different story.

STORYTELLING

If you had a fear and I told you it would never ever come true and you could erase it from your mind forever, would you be interested in hearing how that works? Sorry, can't promise that. But if I told you that what you're worrying about will come true only about 10-20% of the time, would you spend as much time worrying over it as you have been? Those are pretty weak odds. But they say that what we spend our time worrying about comes to pass only about 10-20% of the time. What a bunch of time we waste in worrying. I don't know if you're like me, but I spend a lot of time on worrying over dumb things that either a) I can't control anyway, or b) don't ever come true.

When I get worked up in a fear now, I do something simple but radical: I change the outcome of my fears by telling myself a different story. Take each one of your fears you're spending time and energy on and write mini stories with them. When you get to the point in the story of fear or failure, give yourself a different outcome than the one you've created in your head. I'll show you.

Fear (This is mine.)

I've been working on this book for a long time. I've poured my heart and passion into it. I want it to be encouraging and to help people on their journey. I want people to understand that, if they have a dream, they should dig deep and dream big and take the leap.

But…what if this book sucks and people laugh at me behind my back? What if they're like, "Seriously? This is what she was working on all those months? This is *it*?"

Different Story

What if it's great, and people get lots of really helpful stuff out of it and it helps grow their dreams? What if people see the bravery it took to finish a project and they're inspired to take a leap and finish their big project or go for their big dream, too? That would be my best possible outcome.

You see? You can grab your fears at the point they threaten to turn on you and you can overcome them with the power of storytelling. When your fears want to tell you that you can't do this; tell them a different story.

It's not automatic, but it is really simple, and sometimes simple is better. I'll also admit it's not the easiest practice. I've been practicing like crazy all through this book writing process. But the more you practice something, the more natural and automatic it becomes. Try it with some of your fears and see if you can overcome them by telling a different story.

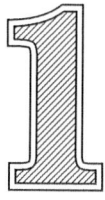

KNOW YOUR VALUES

Before you ever bake a cupcake (or before you ever create whatever it is you're creating), you've got to know exactly what kind of foundation you are building upon. I knew that I had to dream big, dream beyond startup business, but I also knew that if we were going to succeed in the way I would view as successful, we had to be about our values before anything else. When you know your values, your foundation is unshakable no matter what else is happening all around you.

The values I saw as most important were integrity, faith, generosity and family relationships. They were part of our original business model and are at the root of each decision we make about Oh My Cupcakes! present and future.

Those values are not only important to us in our talk, we try to live them out in our walk with each decision, donation, and schedule accommodation we make. I want our staff to be healthy and happy in their own lives and families, because…well because I love them each, individually. But I also want them to have healthy and happy selves and families because it's going to make them healthier and happier at work, too.

TO SHINE GOD'S
LOVE
AND MAKE
PEOPLE
SMILE
...WITH CUPCAKES

This Is How We Do

Our mission statement is "To Shine God's Love and Make People Smile . . . With Cupcakes." It's not just something we print out and stick up on a piece of paper in the hallway that gets creased and dog-eared and wrinkled over time. Our mission statement is displayed proudly for our guests to see. It's front and center as a permanent piece of wall art behind our front counter in our flagship store.

We want to remember these words every day, to live them and breathe them, and we want our guests to see how important this mission is to us. I see our mission statement in three specific parts:

1. **Shining God's love** is the single most important thing we do every day. We shine God's love when we smile. We shine God's love when we greet a guest when they walk in we and make eye contact with them and that smile is so genuine that it reaches our eyes. When a guest comes through our door, we want them to feel like they're valued, like they're the most important person in the world. One of our staff said it best once when she said, "People should feel like a guest walking into our home instead of a customer walking into our store." Isn't that gorgeous? That's why we don't call people customers, we call them guests.

2. **Making People Smile**: People should be happy when they get a cupcake. You've heard that saying, "You can't be sad when you're holding a cupcake"? We sure hope you're not sad. We want to see people smile and to create moments of joy and delight when a guest gets a delivery or looks into the box to see a special order that was prepared just for them.

3. **. . . With Cupcakes**: Cupcakes are the third part of our mission statement. They're actually the least important; shining God's love and making people smile are the two most important things we do. Cupcakes? They're just the delivery vehicle for that love and those smiles. But come on . . . if we're delivering love and smiles, that delivery vehicle has got to be spectacular. It's why we bake from scratch. It's why we really do bake with love. We've got to create an outstanding product and have crazy attention to detail and excellence. Detail matters so much. Our guests get our very best, because of the first two parts of our mission statement.

Business is really just a subset of life. The way you lead, manage and operate your business is a direct reflection of the way you act, think, and treat people in your personal relationships. When people walk through our doors, we want them to feel warmly welcomed. I think that's what God would do, and that's how we hope to shine His love.

Integrity: A Surprisingly Great Flavor in Cupcakes

One of our core values is integrity, so important to the foundation of Oh My Cupcakes!, that we use it as an interview question:

"What does integrity mean to you?"

Webster's says that integrity is: *The quality of being honest and fair. A firm adherence to a code of especially moral or artistic values; incorruptibility.*

When we ask that interview question, we've gotten some surprising answers. You guys, people do not know what integrity means. I don't mean that flippantly. I don't mean to sound like a cranky old guy shaking his fist and grumbling that he doesn't know what this world is coming to . . . I mean people really don't understand the dictionary definition of integrity. When we've asked that question we've gotten answers like, "integrity means having good ideas," or "it means teamwork," or "knowing that you've worked hard on something and you can be satisfied."

While those are all great things, that's not integrity.

If there's a core value that's a foundational part of your business, it's pretty important that people understand it fully. If I tell someone that I have an expectation of integrity but they don't understand what it means, how can I expect them to follow it? That disconnect between expectation and understanding will lead to failure and disappointment on one or both of our parts.

I look for people who breathe integrity. Where it's a quality so inherent, you don't put it on like a shirt before you come to work in the morning but rather it breathes warmly within the cells of your skin and hair and into the marrow of your bones. You wear it inside and out. It means you don't cut corners. It means that even if the frosting bag is running empty and you've got just a few cupcakes left to frost, you take the extra time to refill it and don't skimp or "skinny out" the frosting on the last few cupcakes. It means you don't take the easy way out, even if you're the only one who will ever know. It means you do hard things, or inconvenient things even when you don't want to. It means if you make a mistake, you step forward and raise your hand and say, "yeah, that was me, my bad." Integrity shows you can be trusted, and the integrity of each individual protects the integrity of the whole team.

We have a lot of processes and procedures and kitchen tricks we've learned over the years. They've all been learned through trial and error; and sometimes the error has been painful and costly. You can't blame me if don't want to just give those processes away, right? They're just little things, but so many little things have piled up over nearly six years now that have created a mountain and made us who we are. The little things have become pretty big. It takes a person of integrity to understand how important and meaningful all those little things really are. When the Cupcake Ninjas help protect our information, sure they're protecting me, but they're also protecting each person on the team. They're taking care of each other, you know? We're a stronger team because of the integrity we share.

Integrity is so important to Oh My Cupcakes!, in our company handbook I write, *"your high level of integrity is one of the core values upon which you were hired. Thank you for remaining dedicated to it each day!"* With this couple of sentences, I am doing two things:

1. Choosing to believe that a person lives up to our high standards of integrity.

2. Setting a specific tone that integrity is an expectation; it's not optional.

Sometimes believing the best in others and laying out an expectation of integrity is not enough. Gosh it's difficult

Luke 16:10

If you are faithful in little things, you will be faithful in large ones. But if you are dishonest in little things, you won't be honest with greater responsibilities.

when the expectation of integrity isn't being met. It feels gross and icky and it's usually painful. Sometimes people just don't possess the same set of values. Sometimes major decisions need to be made swiftly for the good of the entire team. We've been at that decision-laden crossroads before in the life of Oh My Cupcakes!, and we will surely be there again because people are just . . . well, people, and we are *all* just really messy sometimes.

A crossroads will likely come in the life of your business where steps will have to be taken to protect your own dreams and to protect the rest of the team and the example they see being modeled. It's not fun, and even as I'm writing this I'm saying a little prayer for that time when you will inevitably reach that crossroads yourself. Integrity is not "doing what's easy," it is "doing what's right," even when it doesn't feel good. That's why you put values in place at your foundation, (you and I are going to work through doing this for your own dream or business) so that when you come to a crossroads the decision-making process is easier. It might not make it hurt any less, but you'll lose less sleep over the decisions when they need to be made.

Integrity is just one block in our foundation. We're also guided by values like faith, serving, generosity and family relationships.

Faith: Inviting God in Before We Invite Our Guests In

Because of the words of our mission statement and our commitment to be closed on Sundays, people ask us all the time if we are a "religious" business. Man, I hate that question. I feel like I'm being set up. Not everyone is this way, but sometimes people throw the words out, head tilted slightly to the side and breath held, waiting for my answer.

I never feel like I'll have the "right" answer to that question. I feel like no matter what I say, if you're the judgey, churchy type, you're going to return my words to me the first time I do something you don't approve of (and just give me time, I will) and serve them to me on a platter of judgment and reproach. Humans are all imperfect and wired to disappoint and given enough time, I promise that I will disappoint you.

What I can tell you is this: I see God's hand in every step of the creation and growth of this business. I see Him every day when we complete orders that seem impossibly large with a staff that seems impossibly small. I know He's right there when we go through unexpected turnover and I'm hanging my head and feeling defeated . . . and just the right people walk through the door and apply for the open positions every single time. I need Jesus . . . oh how I need Jesus. I love God and I want to shine that love onto others. But the God of my universe might look different than the God of your universe, and you know what? I love you, honor you, respect you and accept you fully for believing whatever it is that you believe. In fact, I'd like to have a conversation with you and learn more about why you believe what you believe. Not so I can try to change you, but so I can learn more about you. I want to learn what you know and how you came to know it. I want to learn more about this whole big world and all of us who are floundering around, miserably and wonderfully and beautifully, trying to make sense of it. I want you to feel the love, honor, respect and grace when you walk through our doors that I think God shows to all of us each day.

To me, shining God's love and making people smile with cupcakes is about putting all of the love and positivity we can into creating delightful treats, and then passing them along to others with a smile and without any shred of that churchy judgment. (How can I judge you when I'm so far from perfect?) That's what faith means to me, and what it means when I say that faith is one of our values.

Invited; Not Expected

We start our day with a daily devotional and prayer. I think God is always within Oh My Cupcakes!, but I still think it's important to pause and invite Him in before we invite our guests through our doors. We invite our staff to come to devotions and prayer, but they're not expected to come; everyone has a choice. We also do a little team building with a fun question like "what was your best part of yesterday?" or "what's the best gift you ever received?" or "if you had any superpower, what would it be?" The intentional time we spend together at our little morning meeting helps us look each other in the eye and smile at one another. We cry together sometimes and see each other as people, not just as coworkers. If I'm leading the meeting, we usually go long because I get a little talky.

In addition to my faith in God, faith to me means believing that the best is yet to come; that our best days are still ahead. No matter what faith looks like to you, if you've got a dream you're dreaming, experience has taught me that faith better be one of your building blocks. They don't call it a "leap of faith" for nothing . . . it's not called a "leap of certainty." If you've got a dream you're building, there are bound to be a lot of unknowns ahead of you. Believe the best is ahead, and surely it will be.

You Can Give a Lot With Cupcakes: Generosity

I want to leave a legacy. I think our legacy has a lot to do with what we give away at Oh My Cupcakes! We've worked hard, but God has given us a lot . . .like, a LOT. I think it's both our responsibility and honor to find ways to effectively give to our community whenever we can. We get donation

GIVE

Grace

GIVE

Mercy

AND WORK WITHIN

Kindness

requests multiple times each day and while I wish we could give to every group, (you guys, I'm the worst at saying no) it just isn't possible.

We got focused to make the best impact and created a kind of umbrella over which we cover our donations. We give to organizations that support childhood hunger, homelessness, and the working poor within our community. We also created an endowment with Children's Miracle Network/Cure Kids Cancer and sponsored a room in our local children's hospital. There are no words to express the joy I receive from being able to make a genuine difference in people's lives and wellbeing, simply because of cupcakes. I think of families bringing their children to the children's hospital, maybe scared, and certainly not within their comfort zone. My heart swells with happiness and pride to know that we helped to sponsor one of the rooms there. God did that. Our cupcake ninjas did that. *Cupcakes* did that. Pinch me. It's pretty incredible.

Just like I couldn't determine which values were most important to you, I can't tell you which organizations you might decide to support. I can only tell you which ones I saw had a great need in our community and the ones which spoke to my heart back in the founding days.

Give grace, give mercy, and work within kindness. Know which values you want your business to be founded upon, and hold tightly to those values as you filter through the tough decisions that need to be made.

Our founding verse

Proverbs 16:3

Commit your work to the Lord and your plans will succeed.

Have you ever taken time to identify which values are important to you? If you're a little stuck or overwhelmed, here are a few to get you started. There may be others that are not on this list that are important to you, so feel free to add as you like.

What values are important to you?
(Circle the ones that speak to you the loudest.)

Honesty	Fun	Love
Loyalty	Family	Truth
Commitment	Faith	Hope
Passion	Engagement	Care
Integrity	Learning	Generosity
Respect	Prosperity	Teamwork
Serving	Relaxation	Others?
Consistency	Flexibility	
Honor	Professionalism	
Reliability	Security	_____
Encouragement	Significance	_____
Community	Optimism	_____
Influence	Spirituality	_____
Creativity	Freedom	_____

Now take the ones you've circled, and write down the top five. Yours may not have been on the list, you may have written them on your own:

1. _____

2. _____

3. _____

4. _____

5. _____

Now narrow it down to three. I know this is tough, because they're all *really* important to you. But if you had to sacrifice all else, what are the top three things you'd need to have in your life, no matter what? Write them here:

1. _____

2. _____

3. _____

Hey! Nice job. You've just identified the values that are most important to you. These are the things that shape your life. They've probably been shaping it already, even if you haven't been fully conscious of it. Now you can consciously put those values into the foundation of your business as you grow your dream.

Pause here for a second and reflect:

What values are so *important* to you that you want them to be a foundation for your business?

_____

_____

_____

_____

How can you live these values out in your business each day?

_____

_____

_____

_____

_____

_____

Putting "Know Your Values" at the beginning was totally on purpose, even though I'm worried you'll think I'm being preachy. I'm not trying to be preachy, I'm just trying to get across to you the importance of having *values* under everything you do. You're putting a foundation under the home you're about to build. You want it firm, so it doesn't fall when the first little breeze comes along. You want your foundation rooted in what's important to you so that when things get tough, you'll remember why you're doing this in the first place. Values are your guiding principles that help you accomplish your mission. Values help form your vision, and vision leads you to your *purpose*. We're going to talk more about vision just ahead, and about my purpose and your purpose coming up in the chapter called "Know Your Purpose" (clever, right?) so hang on, ok?

KNOW YOUR VISION

Let's jump in our wayback machine for a minute and head back to a time before Oh My Cupcakes! existed. It was early 2009. I had enjoyed a ten-year radio career. I was beginning to have those rumblings: you know, the "there's more than this that I'm supposed to be doing with my life," feeling. But overall, I was comfortable. I enjoyed radio. In fact, I'd say there were parts of radio that I was still quite passionate about. I knew there was something more, but was I ready to make a change yet?

There was only one thing that could have gotten me to leave my comfort zone: an offer of a position that would allow me to pursue my purpose in life, one where I could encourage women and help them grow forward. I'm passionate about helping women, and so I made a big decision and left my comfortable radio career in May 2008 for a Women's Ministry position at a large and thriving church in my city. I really wanted to finish well, so I gave a six week notice to my radio group.

Four weeks into my notice during the same time frame in which I was training my mid-day replacement, I was called into a meeting at the church. Even going into the meeting, something felt "off" ahead of time. Behind closed doors that Tuesday in May, the church pastor and leadership staff told me not to panic, but they had made some decisions to change things around and to eliminate the paid position in Women's Ministry at the church. They assured me that a position would be found for me somewhere within the church and I still had a job, but it wouldn't be in the same capacity it was originally offered.

The two hour meeting was grueling on so many levels and the afternoon dragged on. Some healing has happened but I will always have the scars of that meeting. I was in shock as I got behind the wheel of my little white Pacifica after that meeting and started driving, then finally pulled off into a McDonald's parking lot and broke down sobbing.

There was no getting my old job back, but now my new job was being taken away. I was filled with grief. I was still good at radio, it's not like I was unhappy in my career. I wouldn't have left my job for *anything* other than Women's Ministry. My replacement had already been found and I knew there was no going back to what was before. I was angry. I was devastated. What was this all about? What was the lesson in all of this?

During those summer months of 2009, I concentrated on spending as much time as I could with my kids and worked part time at the church. I did a lot of data entry. I did some event planning when there were events. I did a little writing and editing for church newsletters and communications when they needed it. Mostly I did a lot of soul searching and questioning.

I look back over that time of initial uncertainty of the job being pulled out from under me and in that time it was so painful. I now know I never would have left a job I loved (radio) for anything other than the promise of something much better (Women's Ministry.) I would likely never have jumped off the cliff and taken a leap of faith to start a new business venture on my own, so I think God had to give me a little nudge, a gentle little push. I want to be clear: it did not feel gentle or nudging at the time. It felt like an unexpected kick, a freefall I was not prepared for, and for a few moments it felt like I was kicking and screaming the whole way, (all while trying to be diplomatic and graceful and keep my cool about it.) Have you been there? Are you there now, in the middle of a life-change you did not ask for?

During this freefall, I found some measure of comfort and contentment in trying out new cupcake recipes and frosting techniques. I baked cupcakes for my coworkers at the church. I searched websites of other cupcake shoppes across the country and learned their unique stories and specialties. I did a little freelance writing to piece together some meager income. I took afternoon picnics with my kids at Falls Park and remembered the simple gift of my breath. I spent my free time learning about regulations for commercial food preparation, made phone calls to potential mentors (more on that coming up) and soaked up all the knowledge I could. I took seminars on how to start a new business. I took walks on the bike trails with my kids, baked more cupcakes, and gave them away to friends and family.

Visioning What Could Be

I have a vision board at my house. I don't hang it over my bed and look at it every day like Oprah says to do. Mine has been propped up against a wall for a while now but that doesn't mean I love it any less, it's just how I roll with it. It's colorful and creative and ripped and wrinkled in places and pretty messy. A little like me, I guess.

All you need
is
Love
and
Cupcakes

It's filled with action words and declarations like This is Your Year for Miracles! and quotes I've cut out of magazines, things I might scrawl hastily on a piece of paper, (You are more than enough) some concrete goals I've set for my life, things that just speak to me for one reason or another, scripture verses, and some Dove chocolate wrappers with deep life wisdom I want to be sure to keep forever. I hang reminders on it to be gentle with myself and talk to myself like I'd talk to someone I love. (More on that inner voice and how she talks to me later.) I've even got pretty clothing tags pinned onto that board from special things I've purchased. My vision board is scattered and yet it's a perfect compilation of all that I am. I look at it from time to time, pull things off that no longer apply, and add new things to it. It's a great reminder not only of where I'm going, but how far I've already come.

There's a piece of paper on my vision board that I've left up for years because it still resonates today. When I first wrote those words on the piece of paper, I jotted down the date I was writing them. The date was 7-19-09. The piece of paper is unremarkable in itself, a half page torn hastily from a yellow legal pad, simple blue ink from a ballpoint pen. Those who know me well know that I rarely use ballpoint pens, and even more rarely do I use boring old blue or black ink. But this time I did. The paper wasn't important and the ink wasn't either. The words themselves are what held such power. The words say, "God wants to do amazing things with my life, and I am ready for the challenge."

I wrote that right after I had been kicked off the cliff. I wrote that just after a Women's Ministry position had come and gone at the church. I wrote that just as I was discovering cupcakeries as the new and growing trend. Every time I look at that piece of paper, I remember exactly how I felt when I wrote those words on 7-19-09. I felt like I was "on the cusp." I was filled with passion and motivation and I was ready to go.

See, for a year or more before any of this transitional stuff, I had felt that God was preparing me for something; that I was on the cusp of something huge. The trouble was, I wasn't entirely sure what it was and I felt frustrated because it all looked so big and looming and I didn't quite understand what it was about. I was going *crazy* with wondering and not knowing what I was supposed to be doing. I was very settled into my career and just had *that feeling*: I want to be doing something else. The feeling like: *I don't know exactly what it is, but I know this isn't it.* Have you ever had that feeling? I had begun to create a vision, but my vision was super blurry. It wasn't yet clear.

Can you relate? Have you been there? Are you there now, even as you're reading these words? If you're there right now, in that space of feeling "on the cusp," I wish I could tell you the exact steps I took, and tell you exactly how the vision became clear to me. I can't. But what I can tell you is I prayed a lot and I gave things time. The journey I took was not the journey I expected to take, nor is it the same one you will take.

That year for me was a journey of addition and subtraction: time + desperation . . . comfort - routine . . . decisions compounded by challenge and unrest. Sometimes those are unwanted but very necessary ingredients to make vision become clear.

Time + the situations which had been placed around me, paired with the subtraction of the radio career I had held close for so many years caused my vision to gradually come into focus.

For a variety of reasons I never found my place at the church (duh, right?), and after about six months or so, I told them I was pursuing writing and cupcakes on my own. I didn't know what it looked like, but I knew it was right. It was so scary. I was leaving the certainty of the paycheck I was receiving at the church for complete uncertainty. Even so, my fear was supplanted by a drive, a fire in my belly like I hadn't felt in a long time.

The things I had originally thought I was *supposed* to be doing (Women's Ministry) had fallen apart, and the things having to do with cupcakes were beginning to fall into place. I was more certain than ever that this was my intended path.

Once it became clear this "cusp of something big" I had been feeling for so long was all about cupcakes, my vision for everything I wanted Oh My Cupcakes! to be also came into crystal clear focus. I became singular-minded. I not only knew how I wanted people to feel when they would eventually come into the store, but I knew what I wanted the experience to be like from beginning to sweet, delightful end. I was researching other cupcake shops in my spare time and knew the things I liked about other shops I'd visited and things I didn't care so much for. I knew I wanted the store to have a vintage feel, like walking into June Cleaver's kitchen, where you'd feel like mom had just whipped up a batch of cupcakes from scratch (probably while wearing pearls and a frilly apron).

I wanted people to be able to return to a simpler time, where the cares of the world could melt away when they walked in the door and they could get wrapped up in the experience of delighting in a moment of luxury. "Just a cupcake shop?" Never. My grandiose dreams were becoming *clear vision* and that vision was taking on depth and texture and life. I wanted Oh My Cupcakes! to be so much more.

I wanted us to be:

> All about excellence, and about giving the guest more than they expect.

> A flavor experience like none other, from first impression to last, delicious crumb.

> About the little things, the tiny details like a perfectly tied bow that looks the same every single time.

> About generosity, beginning with how we serve our product. Giving the guest more than they expect and never skimping on size to save money.

> About buying local whenever possible.

> A values-based business, built on things like family and generosity, faith and kindness.

> A business known for our community involvement. Not just known for donations we'd make, but also for roll-our-sleeves-up service and helping others.

> A place where relationships would be built. A place where people would feel like lingering over a cupcake and coffee.

My vision has depth and detail. But the funny thing about vision is, eventually you have to act upon it. I had laid as much groundwork as I could. It was time to get moving.

Ladies and Gentlemen . . . Meet Brianna

Back when Oh My Cupcakes! was just beginning, four friends sat on a blanket at Lifelight (a Christian music festival) in September of 2009. Me, CW, Brianna and her husband Jared.

I knew Brianna from church and from hanging out, and I knew she was kind of a baking rock star. I shared my cupcake dream and vision with her, and asked her if she wanted to come along for the ride. She said yes. Jared was in the process of buying a fledgling new business just as I was starting Oh My Cupcakes! They had two tiny littles, their youngest was about six weeks old when we started baking in that old commercial kitchen. I couldn't pay Brianna any wage back then, so I would just pay her daycare bill each week when she would come to the kitchen and bake cupcakes with me.

As we sat on this blanket on the side of a hill at Lifelight talking about dreams ahead, Jared said something like, "I think someday Oh My Cupcakes! will be able to support you and your family, and my business will be able to support me and my family." I smiled and said, "Wow, you really think so?" but to be honest, we were baking about four dozen cupcakes a week on special request back then. I had big dreams, but in that moment I thought he was a tad delusional.

Listen . . . I know I keep telling you to dream big, and to think further than six months into business, but I recognize how difficult that is at the beginning. I wanted Oh My Cupcakes! to be a legacy-creating business, but it was a challenge for me to make the connection from heart to head . . . from *want to* to *believing* it could be so big it could sustain my whole family's livelihood.

I wanted to believe great things. But . . . to support my entire family with cupcakes? That seemed pretty far-reaching right in the moment. A nice thought, but lofty.

I've learned my dreams and my vision can only take me so far. When I feel something purposed strongly in my heart, when I know I'm on the right path, I've learned God's plans really are so much bigger than mine. I felt I was making the right decision by taking the position in Women's Ministry when it was offered to me. What if I hadn't acted on it? Think where Oh My Cupcakes! would be if I had stayed back in radio instead of taking that leap? Nowhere at all, as far as I can figure out. Now think where Oh My Cupcakes! would be if that position had worked out just like I thought it was going to? Still nowhere. Sometimes that gentle nudge, the kicking off the cliff, the kicking and screaming freefall is just what you need to get your vision focused and your dreams in action. So if you're in the middle of feeling like you're unsure, and unhappy about it just now, know that it's ok. I understand, and I know you can get out of it. And sometimes what looks like the worst thing actually does turn out to be the best thing.

Our staff of Cupcake Ninjas numbers right around 30 now, and since Oh My Cupcakes! opened officially over five years ago, we've helped support not just my family, but many families.

Have you ever gotten the little kick off the cliff?

How did it feel at the time?

_____

_____

_____

_____

_____

Can you see the bigger picture yet, or are you still in the middle of trying to figure out the lesson in all of it?

_____

_____

_____

_____

_____

KNOW YOUR PURPOSE

Hey, I've got a question for you. It's kind of a big one. What in the world are you doing here? Do you know? On this big ol' watery planet? Any clue? And what am I doing here? Though my answer changes a little big as I get older and as time goes by, I identified some years ago, what my purpose was here on this earth. I wasn't even looking for it, I was just driving to an abuse survivor's group one Sunday afternoon, and I was in prayer about the hours ahead when all of a sudden I got these words:

My Purpose Statement

To use my experiences, skills, and talents to help people. To grow spiritually and personally trough my vocation as well as through personal growth exercises. To inspire women to grow themselves, ensuring them that no matter their circumstances or their past, they can grow into beautiful, strong, and empowered women.

My Purpose Statement:

To use my experiences, skills, and talents to help people. To grow spiritually and personally through my vocation as well as through personal growth exercises.

To inspire women to grow themselves, ensuring them no matter their circumstances or past, they can grow into b strong, and empowered

I scribbled them down on a piece of paper as soon as I pulled into the parking lot at my destination, and then I later typed them onto the paper shown here. (Nice font, right? And you like the scrapbook scissors I used on the edge? Fancy.)

These words sum it up. This is what I'm doing here, on this big ol' watery planet. It's what I want to be about in my life. It's my motivation. It's my why. It's the thing I was put on this earth to do. It's my *purpose*.

But I hope when you read that, it doesn't just look like a bunch of words on a page; they're all very specific to what I want to be about. Let me break it down for you and show you what I mean:

"*To use my experiences, skills, and talents to help people.*" I've been through some things in life. Some have been good, some not so good. I don't want any of those experiences (either positive or negative) to go to waste. I want to be bold enough to share the painful stuff with people and let them know they can get through it and there's beauty on the other side. I want to be humble enough to share the joyous stuff I've been gifted with and to show others how grateful I am for this life that God's given to me. I want to use the experiences I've had to help others.

Also, I've got *skills*, sister. (Gifts from God.) Don't you forget it. And talents. (Also given by God) and I don't want to waste those skills or talents, either. I want to use all that I've been given to help people. It sort of goes back to knowing your values, and *helping people* is something that's always been really important to me.

Next up, "*To grow spiritually and personally through my vocation as well as through personal growth exercises.*" Again, does it just sound like a bunch of jargon? I hope not.

To me it means I want to keep growing, keep learning, keep seeking a higher path of spirituality and to see that my vocation (whatever my job is) supports that growth just as much as anything I do outside of work. For example, I love to write, and I love to learn about writing. So I look for opportunities to go to writer's conferences, attend poetry readings or to teach writer's workshops to others, just to connect with others and stay creatively inspired.

"To inspire women to grow themselves, ensuring them that, no matter their circumstances or their past, they can grow into beautiful, strong, and empowered women." That's really what I want to be about, you know? I want to help people, particularly women, understand that it doesn't matter what your past is like; where you've been or what you've been through in your life . . . your choices going forward are yours and yours alone. You can grow into anything you want to be. I'm so passionate about helping women discover their voice and their power because of the difference it made in my own life once I found my voice, it's really what I want to spend my life doing. I feel like this is my life's work; my purpose.

When I'm feeling creatively stifled, I look over my purpose statement and ask myself, "Well, are you doing any of these things? Are you still using this purpose statement as a filter for your decision-making?" If my answer is no, if I'm not using my purpose statement as my filter, then I can figure out the reason for my restlessness pretty quickly. If I'm not living within my purpose, I'm not usually a very happy camper. Odds are also pretty high if I'm not living within my purpose, I'm probably saying "yes" to a lot of stuff that isn't really meant for me, which means there isn't a lot of time left over for the stuff that God has planned JUST for me.

There's something pretty key to this purpose statement stuff. I'm not sure if you caught but I want to be sure you do: *my purpose statement doesn't point to any specific job or vocation.*

It doesn't say I have to be a teacher or a painter or a banker or a baker to make live out my purpose. It just lays out the things I want to do with my life. So many times I see people struggling to figure out their purpose and they're wrapping all of this thought up in *what* they're supposed to do with their life, when I think we really should be trying to figure out *who* we are supposed to be and what we are supposed to be *about*. We can be *who* we want to be anywhere, in any job we do. So if you're trying to figure out if starting this business or pursuing this dream is really where God wants you or if it's really where you're supposed to go, ask yourself, "is it what I want to be about?" We're going to work together and create a purpose statement for you and for your life and see if it helps.

Here's mine again: "*To use my experiences, skills, and talents to help people. To grow spiritually and personally through my vocation as well as through personal growth exercises. To inspire women to grow themselves, ensuring them that, no matter their circumstances or their past, they can grow into beautiful, strong, and empowered women.*"

I left my radio job to do Women's Ministry at a church. I thought the job in Women's Ministry fell right into the parameters of my purpose statement, and it definitely did. So, doesn't baking cupcakes seem like a hard right turn away from Women's Ministry? Might seem like it from an outsider's perspective, but when I look back over the words of my personal Purpose Statement, I can tell you that I live my purpose statement at Oh My Cupcakes! every day. I've been lucky enough to share tears and dreams and deep conversations in my office and in the kitchen and over coffee with so many women who have come through the doors of Oh My Cupcakes!, I can't even count. When we do devotions in the morning and share prayer, I seek a higher spirituality and learn from those around me. I get to encourage and empower women, to use my skills and talents to help people, and to continue to grow myself each day. I get to live my purpose statement which is about talents and growth and ministry, but every day looks a lot like cupcakes and frosting and conversation. Make no mistake: you can live your purpose whenever and wherever you're at, as long as you know what your purpose is.

Do you?

How many of you are thinking, "Aw crap, I knew you were going to ask that question. Hell to the no I don't know what my purpose is. I barely know what socks I have on right now."

It's ok if you don't. Most people's purpose does not come to them suddenly on a Sunday as they're driving across town. But as you're building your business and growing your dream, you really want to think about a very important thing: *why am I building it in the first place?*

I don't want to throw in the cliché "hate to burst your bubble" phrase, but if you're getting into business to make money, I hate to burst your bubble. (Did it. Couldn't be helped. Had to be said.) Call me crazy, but I don't think building a business or growing a dream should be about making money. Money may be a nice byproduct of your dream, but what if it isn't? What if you struggle for years and you don't make a dime? (Thanks, Suzy Sunshine, right?) But what if that's not the plan for you? You need a purpose bigger than material things. You need a reason to do what you do that supersedes personal status or a bigger house or financial gain.

Go back to your values. Which ones did you circle? Which ones did you narrow it down to? Which ones were your top three? Why did they ring true to you as something you want to be about?

Rewrite your top three values from page 33 here:

_____

_____

_____

Now let's talk about the things you are passionate about. What makes you tick? I'm not even talking about passion within the business you're building (although if your personal passion and your business are super-directly linked and tied together — great!) These are your personal passions in life. What are they?

Write them here:

_____

_____

_____

_____

Combine your values and your passion. Create a purpose statement for your life that cements your values and your passion neatly together and tells the world what you are about. Think of your passions, your values, and the contributions you want to make to the world as well as the learning or growth you still want to make as a person going forward. You can add in any or all of those pieces into your Purpose Statement.

My Purpose Statement:

_____

_____

_____

_____

_____

_____

Nice job! Have you ever done anything like that before? How does it feel? Truly I don't think there are a large number of people on this earth who know their purpose, so you're in a select and awesome group. Pat yourself on the back! This isn't easy stuff, but you're doing it.

Next we're going to think about this business, this dream you're building. Let's talk a little about why you're doing what you're doing. I told you my purpose statement for my life, but our mission statement for Oh My Cupcakes! is different. Our mission statement: "To shine God's love and make people smile . . . with cupcakes." As important as my personal purpose statement is to me, our mission statement is to our business. It guides our decisions and helps lead our growth. When we strip everything else away, it's what we want to be about.

Our mission statement means so much to us because sometimes cupcakes and frosting and special moments get trumped by scheduling headaches and cranky customers and deliveries that don't go right. The fun sort of gets sucked right out of the cupcake. Having a mission statement keeps us focused on the right thing instead of the headaches and hassles. It reminds us what we are about and why we are doing what we're doing. I wouldn't recommend being in business without identifying *why* you're there in the first place. When you peel everything else away, shining God's love and making people smile with cupcakes is *all* we are there to do each day.

Why are you doing what you're doing?
Create a mission statement for your business:

_____

_____

_____

_____

_____

_____

Take it one step further. Let's put those values into our every day. I told you Integrity, Faith, Family and Generosity were our guiding values. How do we live those out every day at Oh My Cupcakes?

Integrity: Taking responsibility for mistakes. Committing not to cut corners, even if it costs us more. Telling the truth.

Faith: Meeting for devotions in the morning or sharing our prayers with each other. Believing the best is still ahead.

Family: Providing accommodating schedules. Welcoming people's families and kids when they stop in to say hello. We love families at Oh My Cupcakes!

Generosity: Random Acts of Cupcakes (we GIVE AWAY cupcakes to random people on the street and tell them to have a great day.) We do little giving celebrations a couple of times a year where we give away crazy amounts of money all through our city. We want to make a positive difference in our corner of the world. When we mess up on an order, we give back more than what we messed up. For example, if we got a $20 order wrong, we might offer a gift certificate for $30 or re-do a delivery but include some extra cupcakes in the box.

Decide how you will live out your values within the context of your business each day. **Write it out here:**

Purpose. Mission. Values. These are the things that will keep you strong when you want to quit. Hold them close to your heart, but share them boldly with everyone you meet so they know what your business stands for and what you're all about beyond the product or service you provide. Don't lose sight of your purpose, your mission or your values. These ideals will keep your bones and your body moving when you think you can't go on anymore.

KNOW YOUR WORTH

I'm not telling our story chronologically, but instead telling you the points I think are really key and sprinkling in bits of how we got from there to here, so I hope you're sticking with me. There are a few things we may have changed or altered a bit along the way as we came to know what the business and our guests needed most, but one thing we haven't wavered on: we rarely discount our product.

I don't mean it to sound sassy, but I call it the "Coach bag" mentality. I don't buy a Coach bag because it's on sale, I buy a Coach bag because it's a Coach bag and I want it. It's a luxury item and I'm willing to spend money on it. The second you discount your product or service, you devalue it for now and you devalue it for the future.

As I've mentioned, I spent a lot of years in radio. One of the radio groups I was with had a show that ran on Saturday mornings on the AM station called the Caller's Club or something similar to that. It was a show where people could call in and bid on things. A gift certificate to a restaurant, for example. The caller was granted the power to say just how much they wanted to pay for this gift certificate or whatever item it was they were bidding on.

Picture this: "So next up we've got a certificate for Jim's Pizza. It looks like it's for three large pizzas. Now this certificate has to be used all in one visit, and it's for carry out only. How much do you want to bid on this? Do we have a caller on the line?"

Usually one of the first callers would be a woman with a gravely voice who sounded like she had sucked back a pack of Winston's and a shot of OJ for breakfast. "Yeah, hi Dave. Say, can I put any toppings I want to on those pizzas, or do they tell me what kind of pizza it has to be?"

"Let's see here. . .yeah . . .yeah, it looks like you can pick your own toppings. Do you have a bid for me? Is this Cheryl by the way?"

"Haha, yeah it sure is! Yep, it's me. Let's see, I guess I'll give seven bucks for those pizzas."

"Seven bucks? Now Cheryl, this is for *three* large pizzas from Jim's. Not just one."

"Yeah, I know, I was just hoping . . ."

Then the on-air person would set up a few ground rules and say something like, "We're gonna do a minimum bid on this of . . . let's say . . . $16. A minimum bid of $16."

"Ok, well if no one else calls in for more, put me down for $16."

And in the end, a certificate for three large pizzas would usually go to Cheryl for $16 lousy bucks, even though they were worth a heck of a lot more than that. I'm going to let you in on a little secret. In the radio world, in the eye-rolling whispered hallway conversations, we called that show the Plate Licker's Club. I know that's not very nice and it's not a pretty name. But come on . . . it was painful to listen to. It made my ears bleed. Most importantly: it made Jim's Pizza look like it was a cheap piece of . . . pizza. It devalued the product. If Cheryl could get a certificate for three large pizzas for $16 bucks by dialing up a Saturday morning call-in show, would she ever pay $16 bucks for one large pizza by dialing up Jim's pizza on a Tuesday night? Probably not.

Early on I decided that Oh My Cupcakes! wasn't going to be a discount or deal or coupon kind of business. I'm not saying this is the right way or the wrong way to do things, and you might decide something totally different for your business or venture. That's what is so cool about your own venture: you are the decision maker, and you decide what's right for you. I decided it wasn't right for us, and staying true to the value of our product is how we decided to do business at Oh My Cupcakes!

Not only did our business launch in the middle of the Great Recession, but it opened in dead center of the Groupon frenzy. I saw countless businesses jump on the Groupon bandwagon. A business friend of mine who does gorgeous custom cakes did a Groupon for a small cake which was valued at $30 but sold on Groupon for $15. The way Groupon's business model works is this:

Groupon keeps half of that discounted price ($15) and the business keeps half.

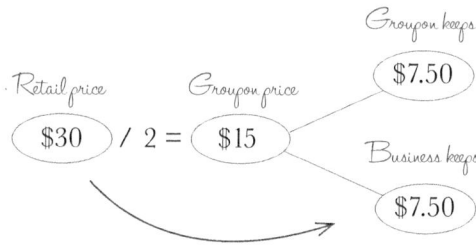

My friend sold her $30 cake for $15, then Groupon took half of that amount ($7.50). My friend sold dozens of those cakes and indeed got exposure to tons of new customers. But for each of those $30 cakes, she took home $7.50. She could barely cover her ingredient cost, and certainly couldn't cover the cost of her time. I hesitate to stereotype a specific type of customer because many of those who buy Groupon deals are great people, but some of the Groupon customers she sold to were just plain pains in the butt. Some of them wanted so much customization or detail work on their $15 cake, they were really asking for a $60 cake. My friend was working her tail off, working all hours of the day and night, to take home $7.50. Did it expose her to new clients? Absolutely. Are some of those clients still today? Probably. Was it worth it? I think she would tell you no way in hell.

Groupon's phone calls were relentless, their telemarketing team was better than any political campaign team in history. Still, I stayed strong and never jumped on the bandwagon. We fielded the calls as graciously and as patiently as possible and never have offered a Groupon, or a DealChicken, or a Spotlight Deal, or any of those other "discount me now, buy me up cheap" offers.

I heard and listened to all of the arguments, I did.

It will give your business great exposure.

It's really a win-win.

It will bring in new business.

I've got a philosophy on the new business these deals bringing in: most of the people buying these certificates aren't people who would have checked us out if our product wasn't discounted. There are always some exceptions of course. But if I discount now, chances are the person who bought at a deep discount won't feel great about paying full price.

You guys, I'm as guilty as anyone else. Example? There are certain craft and home decorating stores that I go into that frequently have entire categories of the store discounted 40-50% off. I love this. Buy all the things! But on the off chance that I need something specific and that category of the store isn't on sale, I almost feel cheated. I get frustrated knowing I need an item today, but it'll probably go on sale next week or maybe I just missed the sale by a day or two. I start to feel entitled to my discount. "Hey, what gives? Can't you do anything about this?" It's totally inappropriate.

What happens in that situation is that I begin to pay more attention to the value of the discount instead of the value of the product. I pay more attention to the sale than I do the worth of the product or item I'm buying.

Worth. What's the worth of your product or service? What's the worth of your time? What is the worth of the hours of research and development and passion you've put into creating this business or venture thus far? What is *your* worth?

In business and in life, you must recognize your worth. You must know your value, and know that if you weren't valuable, you wouldn't be sought out for whatever product or service you are providing. It's so important that you recognize the hard work and effort that goes into all you do and all you've done thus far to create your business. Don't cheat yourself, don't undervalue your contributions, and don't let anyone make you feel bad for the way you've decided to price things or because you won't give them a deal.

YOU ARE WORTHY OF

GREATNESS

AND YOU CAN DO THIS.

Oh honey, this goes for so many things in life, but in business especially, it is so crucial. I have seen women and men alike who, for any number of reasons, seriously undervalue what they do. Sure, in the beginning we all begin with a lack of a portfolio/experience/reputation/street cred.

You know what's cool about life? No matter what your background is, every single one of us started at the bottom when learning our field. Even if you grew up in a family business, you started by learning the basics. If you didn't start at the bottom, you couldn't learn the lessons you need, make the small mistakes you need to make, and most importantly lay the foundation you need to build your skills upon.

So if your business is new (or maybe it's not even a business yet, maybe you're still on the cusp) and you're wondering how to value yourself and don't yet know your worth, please let me give you a gentle word of encouragement: *you are worthy of greatness, and you can do this*. You fake it till you make it and you act like you're a big deal until you *are* a big deal. Present yourself with confidence, like you're someone worth knowing (you are), like you're a business worth doing business with (again, you are) and soon enough you will be a big deal and you actually will know what you're doing.

Is that dishonest? To pretend to be more than you are? Gosh, I'm not a fan of people who put their noses in their air and act like they're better than everyone else. I'm not telling you to act like you're better than anyone else. I'm asking you to square your shoulders with confidence and acknowledge all the good things about yourself. Don't pretend you're better than anyone, but I don't think there's anything wrong with acting like you already are where you hope you'll someday be. Does that make sense? Give yourself some credit, hold your head high and throw a smile on your face. You've already accomplished so much, and from here you're only going to do more great things. I believe in you. How about *you* believe in you, too?

I want to make one more thing clear really quickly. I'm not ever saying you should lie about your accomplishments or embellish the truth of your journey. Always act with integrity. But you know what? Present yourself with poise and hold yourself to the regard with which you want others to hold you. Self-assurance is being confident that you've got a great foundation, a great vision, and a spectacular future ahead of you. Knowing your worth comes from knowing you've got something special now, and you're on your way to being all you're acting like you are right now.

So you work to build that up. In the early days, you might need to do things at a donation or do some projects pro bono to build up your name and reputation, but be clear on what the market value of your service or product actually is and communicate that to your client. Show them on paper just what you'd actually charge for the service or amount of product you're giving them. Let them see it. Down the road, those partnerships you've formed may become profitable for you (that's the hope, right?) and when they become your paying client, they will already have a familiarity with your pricing structure.

Know Your Worth . . . Know Your Limits

Lots of organizations and potential clients present you with amazing opportunities. I find it so difficult to say no to people . . . I really want to be involved in everything. But to protect your company's growth, you need to value your time, know your worth and know your limits. Find organizations that you can become partners with because you see the value in the exposure your client can provide *for you* as well as the service you can provide *for them*. Find organizations and clients you genuinely connect with and enjoy working with. Find places you're passionate about and donate your time and services there.

I heard a great quote from speaker Matthew Kelly, "When we say yes to the stuff that's not for us, we say no to the stuff that God has created *just* for us." Choose carefully. It's ok to say no, even though it feels big and bold and might take your breath away. I *still* worry that if I say no, people won't like me. But that's fear talking. And I've learned to never make a decision out of fear. When I make decisions out of fear, I make the wrong decisions approximately 89.9% of the time. When I make decisions based on our mission statement, our values, based on doing what I think is best for our company going forward, and most importantly based on my *gut*, I rarely get it wrong.

When you know your full value, you'll realize that saying no really means, "This is a great opportunity for someone else, this isn't the best fit for me and my business right now." Be gracious about it when you give either your yes or your no. Be confident. Be firm. And then be content in knowing that you've valued yourself and your business because you know your worth. Showcase your good stuff.

What are you most confident about?

What organizations or types of businesses do you feel a heart connection with?

_____

_____

_____

How can you reach out to them?
Jot down some ideas for ways you can work together that would be mutually beneficial for both of you.

_____

_____

_____

_____

Now let's talk about fears a little bit, and let's move through them. **Write about a time you didn't trust yourself and you made a decision out of fear:**

_____

_____

_____

_____

_____

How did it turn out?

Remember Storytelling? Storytelling is telling yourself a different story when you get to a point of fear or failure when talking through something in your mind.

How can you best use storytelling to help yourself understand that not every opportunity will be the best for you?

5

KNOW YOUR PRODUCT

When beginning a new business, typically you're pretty obsessed with your own ideas about whatever it is you're doing. Is it gourmet cupcakes? Caramels? Fancy dog treats? Auto parts? Whatever your business idea or new venture is, chances are you've spent quite a bit of time obsessing over just how you want to do things.

When I was in the "dreaming and brainstorming" phase of building Oh My Cupcakes!, I spent an insane amount of time on the internet. Like, I really am embarrassed to tell you how much time I spent surfing the web looking at cupcake shoppes across the nation. But what might have looked like me wasting hours of my precious time was actually the act of me gathering super valuable information. I don't know how you best gather and process information, but for me it's by some kind of osmosis. I need to look at things . . . like, a lot of things . . . and then I begin to form thoughts and hypotheses and understandings based upon the mounds and mounds of info I've gathered. Things just click into place for me once I gather tons of facts, that's how my brain works. You might do it differently and hey, that's cool too. Maybe you sit and read with paper and pen and write down specific things as you see them. (Side note, your method is probably way more efficient, because I spend a lot of time saying, "I read something . . . somewhere, one time about that, but now I can't remember where I read it.")

Regardless of your method of research, (and quit judging mine, ok?) you'll want to gather as much information about your product as you can. You've got an awesome product or service you want to offer the world. What makes it awesome? What makes the unique thing that you make . . . unique?

What is it capable of? What are you doing that no one else is? What are other people around the world doing with the same type of product or service you're going to provide?

In addition to the time in front of a computer screen, I also visited as many cupcake shoppes as I could find. This wasn't easy, since there were no cupcake shoppes in South Dakota at the time. Back then, there was one cupcake shoppe in Omaha called Cupcake Island. I visited there a few times, and even called up Ed and Shirley (the business-partner owners) and asked them questions, took them out for lunch to pick their brains, all that kind of stuff. They were a great resource and became quasi-mentors to me. They gave me really helpful information about things they did when they were just starting out, and let me know some things they recommended I should definitely do or most definitely not do based on what they had learned.

When I made that first phone call, they could have hung up on me and refused to answer any of my questions (there were a couple of places I called that did hang up on me), but instead they saw a girl who was just beginning her dream and they decided to help her out. I am forever grateful to Shirley and Ed, and have made a commitment to do the same kindness for others because of the generosity I was shown when I was just starting out.

Cupcake Island wasn't the only gourmet cupcakery I visited. I visited cupcake shoppes in Scottsdale, Phoenix, Kansas City, Dallas, Houston, Cleveland, and back in Omaha after more cupcake places opened there. I visited cupcake shoppes all over the internet. I learned what others were doing. I learned how they presented their product in their stores. I watched how they packaged their cupcakes, what type of boxes they used, how many varieties they kept in the bakery cases at a time, and how their staff treated me as a consumer.

I paid attention to the stores and how they were decorated, how quickly the line moved and how many tables were in each location. Did they have more than one location? How long had they been in business? How many customers were in the dining room on a Saturday morning? Interesting. A Tuesday afternoon? Noted. I got to know my own product in the kitchen through recipes and testing, but I got to know the business of cupcakeries by ~~stalking~~ visiting as many other places as I could.

If you aren't trying to find businesses similar to yours, you're doing yourself and the future of your dream a huge disservice. I've seen some pretty interesting and innovative things people have done with a simple cupcake, things I never would have imagined myself. No, you don't want to be just like them; listen, do not be a copycat. But those visits (either online or in person) gave me gobs of creative information about other cupcakeries who were already in business, doing *the thing I wanted to be doing*. They were already living the dream I was just beginning to breathe life into and create, you know? I saw value in learning from them. I put all the information I had gathered together in my mind (because that's how I do, we've covered this) and then I pulled the best little bits from each of these lovely, faraway places to create Oh My Cupcakes!

Be an original . . . create your own dream . . . but learn from what others are doing and see how that can enhance your ideas and lend to the awesome things you are already doing.

Who do you look up to in the world of whatever it is you create? Who (around the nation or world) is already doing what you want to be doing?

_____

_____

_____

_____

_____

For me, there was Sprinkles Cupcakes™ (duh, right?) Trophy Cupcakes in Houston, and a place in Scottsdale called simply Cupcake. I loved More cupcakes in Chicago and though I can't even put my finger on what the "it" thing was about each of these places, I liked different things about each of them. There are so many more, I could use up another 2,000 words just highlighting all the great cupcake shoppes I've visited. There is so much talent in the world and I love seeing how every individual puts their own spin on theirs. These were my cupcake rock stars.

Today, we do our best to keep innovating. We've done a few things right, we've been blessed and we've had some success but we don't ever want to get stale or boring. Stale and boring is not only bad news for our guests, its bad news for our Cupcake Ninjas because it means they aren't being allowed to play or keep creatively engaged. We love to play in the kitchen. Just yesterday, after I had been at Starbucks writing all day and walked into the Magical Cupcake Kitchen, there were chocolate cake pops with brightly colored sprinkles, new raspberry cheesecakes with a swirl of cream cheese frosting, and gluten-friendly lemon flavors all sitting on a prep table. They are all experiments, new things created just yesterday. It was a play day in the kitchen, and play days in the kitchen make my heart smile. Play days keep us fresh.

At this point in our story, there are other cupcake shoppes in South Dakota and in Sioux Falls. We are careful not to copy what those around us in our area are doing because we want to be as original as possible. It irks me when I see that someone right around the corner has blatantly ripped off a cupcake name that I came up with or a flavor combo we dreamed up in our kitchen, so I want to be sure to stay away from doing the same kind of thing.

We give a glance at what others around us are doing, but now we are nearly six years into business, I keep telling the Cupcake Ninjas, "Hey, we run our own race." We pay attention to the other guys enough to know they're there, but we are responsible for running our own race. We don't get distracted or spend our energy worrying over what they're doing. Run your own race. It's the best one you'll ever run, and the only one.

We pay attention to the important tasks of today, but keep looking off into the distance and asking ourselves what's next. It seems like the trends on the east and west coasts are usually a year or two ahead of us here in the Midwest, so we kind of keep an eye on what's hot out there, then try to shape our direction and our future planning accordingly. Someone's using lavender as an ingredient? Interesting . . .

let's see if it works for us. Savory cupcakes are the new thing, with bleu cheese instead of cream cheese in the frosting? Hmmm. I wonder if that could work here. There's a great saying, "Take what you like and leave the rest."

We take in those bits of information we gather by looking at what the other guys far away are doing, and then we decide what works for us. If it fits for us, great. If not, we filter out the rest. Is this all getting big and overwhelming to you? Are you losing your sense of "I can do this"? Maybe instead you're thinking, "Back the truck up, sister, I don't have time for all this researchy stuff . . . aint nobody got time for that." (So researchy is really not a word? Who knew?)

Hang on a second. I want to be sure I don't scare you and I want you to remove the word "research" (er . . . researchy) from your brain here, because research sounds so structured and boring and time-consuming. What you're doing when you're checking out other like-minded businesses is time-consuming, yes, but if you're passionate about your product or service, you'll find it to be pretty fun. Engaging. Creative. Maybe you're doing this informal research already; spending hours obsessing over those who have gone ahead of you and you're saying, "Oh this research thing? Don't you worry . . . I've totally got this."

I just want you to stay open to all of the possibility out there, keep your mind aware of all the potential ideas and avenues down which you could take your idea, and be excited to embark upon this journey of looking into what other like-minded people all around the world are doing.

Hey, you have it way easier than I did. Back in my day, we only had the internet! And it was dial up! (I joke, kind of.) When Oh My Cupcakes! began, I didn't have the benefit of fancy social-sharing apps like Instagram, Twitter and

Pinterest. Isn't it crazy to think that all of those were created within the past six years? (Twitter was actually created in 2006 but didn't really take off until 2009 or so.) Now, it's easier than ever to see what people all around the world with the same interests as you are doing with those interests, or to hear what they're saying about them. If you've got a little bit of tech savvy, your search is as simple as a hash tag or @ symbol.

Social sharing sites aside, don't ever underestimate the importance of a personal contact. Pick up the phone once in a while and ask someone if you can get into their brain or take them out to lunch and try and learn a thing or two. Social sites and the internet are great for gathering information and ideas, but there is no replacement for genuine human contact.

What businesses or like-minded individuals can you contact to see if they could be a resource for helping you build your dream?

Now think bigger. Who are your real "rock stars" that you think would never return your phone calls? I heard some great advice once, "Make them tell you 'no'." Why don't you give them a call and just see what happens? Make them tell you no.

List out a few of those, "rock star status" possible mentors here.

_____

_____

_____

_____

How can you apply "take what you like and leave the rest" to your business planning?

_____

_____

_____

_____

_____

_____

KNOW YOUR AUDIENCE

From the time I had an original vision about having a gourmet cupcakery, I had a dream it would be in The Bridges at 57th Street. The Bridges at 57th is an exclusive *lifestyle center* type of shopping center on the south side of the city, filled with lovely and like-minded upscale businesses.

In The Bridges you can buy designer clothing for yourself or your spouse, consign your Coach or Burberry so someone else can buy and enjoy them, and while you're in the store you can buy more clothing and accessories because, let's be honest, you can't leave empty-handed. In another store you can buy designer duds for your dog or your cat and scientifically balanced food for Fido or Fifi. Down a few doors you'll find nutritional supplements (for you), next door to them you can get a precision haircut or visit the medical spa upstairs. You can pick up a quality educational toy for your niece or nephew and have it gift wrapped charmingly . . . and on the house.

Walk across the parking lot and you can pick up a great bottle of wine and some gourmet cheese or any other high-end food you might want to serve at your next get-together. In The Bridges at 57th St. you can even have a consultation and set up an appointment to get quality granite countertops installed in your home. The property developer is intentional about the quality rather than the quantity of businesses they attract. The businesses are all complementary, one to the next.

I always had my heart set on The Bridges at 57th. When I first began to dream and to look at property for Oh My Cupcakes! in 2009, I looked at a vacant space in The Bridges. Oh how I wanted that space; you guys it was perfect. It was a space occupied formerly by a meal-prep franchise called Super Suppers and was already outfitted with an exhaust hood, which is super costly in the restaurant world. It had a kitchen in the back, a place for guest seating in the front, a laundry room . . . like I said, it was perfect. Unfortunately it did not have a perfect price tag to meet my budget at that time. I think my perfect price tag at that time was probably "free," and oddly enough, no one was really renting at that price. I tried to crunch numbers and finesse things, but there was just no way to make it work out. I met with an awesome banker named Ryan and we had a good conversation.

"That's a lot of widgets," he said. "No matter if you're selling cupcakes or tchotchkes, they're all widgets, right? If you're selling *anything* at a low price point, you've got to sell a lot of them to make up your expenses each month." He didn't laugh me out of his office, (score) but he helped me see it just wasn't meant to be at that time. I could not afford that space. I was temporarily deflated.

I remember friends at the time saying, "Are you sad? What will you do now? Do you feel like your dream is over?"

Sure I was sad and I was for sure deflated in those few days surrounding the realization that The Bridges spot was not meant to be mine, but I've never been one to easily accept a "no" as a "no." I didn't feel at all like my dream was over.

I never felt like God was shutting the door or saying "no", I felt like He was saying, "not yet." It wasn't yet our time. We weren't ready for The Bridges.

Getting to Know You

Oh but I knew The Bridges. I knew that southern area of town. Not because I lived there, but because I had been doing all I could do to learn about it. When I was doing all of the researchy stuff, looking at cupcake shoppes flung all across the U.S., I was also researching the people who lived in that upscale south side of town. The people who lived in that area were the ones I had identified as the ones I wanted to serve. I knew they would be my customer; my audience. I did demographic research and learned about their household size, their income level, the average age of the homes they lived in, what kind of cars they drove, all the things I could find by simple google searches or by driving through some neighborhoods and just looking at things. That sounds kind of stalkerish, I promise I was not stalking the neighborhood.

When things didn't initially work out in the space in that gorgeous upscale southern side of the city and I couldn't afford the space, my focus *never strayed* from that area of town. Even though Oh My Cupcakes! was first in a kitchen space on the east side of our city, and then within a few months had moved into our downtown location, I never did shift my heart's focus away from The Bridges. God had said, "Not yet," but I always felt that someday we would find our true home in that upscale area.

But I'm getting all ahead of myself. Back to (semi) chronological order here, Melissa, come on.

Let's head downtown.

So it's March of 2010, and the opportunity presented itself for Oh My Cupcakes! to move into a space in our city's charming downtown. We were able to take over the lease from someone who couldn't maintain her space anymore so I always felt like it worked out for both of us: we could help her out of her situation and Oh My Cupcakes! got the pretty spectacular benefit of a cute little storefront. I did love downtown, it offered a camaraderie like I'd never felt before or since. It had an eclectic feel, and we had great parking (which is not always the case with downtown businesses.) We opened our storefront downtown April 1st of 2010, and had a full house. It was the next step in our great ride, and we found our home there for 3 ½ lovely years.

Even though downtown is where our store was located for those 3 ½ years and as strange as it might sound, I never spent time researching the customer who lived around us in the downtown area. I kept laser focus on the southern half of our city. You might think I'm a crazy girl, but I stick to it; I knew my customer was still in that part of our city. When we made deliveries they would often be located in that area of town. Or we would talk to our guest when they visited our downtown location and they'd say things like, "We love you guys, even though we have to drive all the way over here to find you." Our primary customer didn't live downtown, she lived in other parts of town and was driving to get to us. (Our primary customer was a "she," too.) Of course she wasn't exclusive to the southern side of the city, but primarily, our target audience was out there. And that's where I knew someday we would be.

Where does your customer live? Is it a specific area?
(That might not apply to you, but consider it.)

You Talkin' To Me?

I used to do radio. When I started, I did 4 hours on air a week, Saturday afternoons on the hard rock station in town. I was Metal Melissa, and my opening line every show was a sultry, "The lipstick is on, the shoes are off, it's time to rock." (Side note, I really did do my afternoon show barefoot. Loved it.)

Gradually I worked my way up to fulltime nights, then afternoons. I knew my stuff when it came to hard rock. I could tell you when Linkin Park's new album was due out, if Incubus was touring anytime soon, when Disturbed might be hitting the studio again and what side project Tool's Maynard James Keenan was working on. I knew Three Doors Down's hometown, the story behind Theory of a Deadman's band name, (one of my favorite interesting little rock trivia nuggets, ask me sometime and I'll tell you) and if Scott Weiland was in or out of rehab that week. I knew my stuff because that's what my audience wanted to know about. I knew who was listening to me, and I talked about the things the audience wanted to hear.

At home; totally different story. Power Puff girls was on my T.V. 24/7 back then; Bubbles Buttercup and Blossom (and don't forget Mojo Jojo.) I had two little girls (Brandon was born towards the end of my Metal Melissa days) and I was busy being a mom to young girls. I was making homemade Play Doh, helping organize Christmas cookie exchanges and attending preschool programs. And while I didn't completely avoid talking about those types of things on the air, I might mention them only in passing. They were a thin layer to my on-air persona, but I was talking primarily to males, ages 18-34, and carpools and cookie exchanges weren't what my primary listener wanted to hear about.

I knew my audience.

Later in my radio career I moved on to a CHR (Contemporary Hits Radio) station whose target demo was females age 18-40. These women I talked to each day were just like me. On this station, coming up with daily show prep was easy as pie: I just talked about things I was interested in, things that affected my life or a life just like mine. Suddenly cookie exchanges and carpools and preschool programs were totally on-topic. I could talk about makeup and bad hair days, about newsworthy things that I found interesting because likely my audience was going to find them interesting as well. In fact, it was as I was searching for show prep one day that I read a story about gourmet cupcake shops and how they were opening up all across the nation.

Wait, what? A cupcake shop? Where people buy *just cupcakes*? I talked about it on the air that day. And then I became a little obsessed and the rest became history.

Have you taken time to think about who is "listening" to you? Have you considered exactly who is buying what you're selling? *Who* are you going to be serving each day?

Coming up in "Knowing Your Boundaries", I'm going to talk about how, as much as I'd like to, I can't please everyone.

You can't either. You hear that? That's a true statement that you probably understand on a surface level, but I want you to dig a little deeper with me and decide, "Who *am* I going to please?" Consider for a moment who you are trying to reach, who your target audience is, and then we'll dig into how you can try to reach them.

Who is your audience?

Will your audience be primarily male or female?

What are some of your audience's "likes"?

Does considering your audience's interests change how you should talk to them?

What phrases will connect with them when you communicate with them?

Introductions, Please.

I'd like to introduce you to Sarah. (Hi Sarah.) Isn't she pretty? She is. Sarah is 37 years old. She has two kids, (I think they're girls, and I think they have blonde hair, and I totally think Sarah dresses them alike and they get super annoyed by it, but that's just me). The girls are ages six and nine. Sarah works twenty to thirty hours a week, probably in a clinic or office setting. Sarah drives a crossover vehicle like a Honda Pilot or a Chevy Traverse. She has the girls signed up for dance or soccer or some extra-curricular sport which keeps her evenings busy, and she's part of book club or church small group or Bunco or a group that gets her out of the house once in a while for some mommy time of her own but also fills her schedule right up.

Sarah watches HGTV and The Food Network, and she also watches Scandal and Grey's Anatomy. (What the heck? McDreamy???) She was devastated when Parenthood ended and she still doesn't know what to do with herself on Thursday nights. She hits up Facebook multiple times a day like when she's standing in line in the grocery store or while she sits in the parking lot waiting for her daughters' dance class to finish up. She loses hours each week on Pinterest.

Sarah likes to bring treats for her coworkers and celebrate the girls' birthdays at school, but she feels starved for time the way it is. Sarah likes to hit the drive through at Starbucks on her way to work a couple of times a week but she gets irritated by long lines. Not because she's impatient by nature, just because she's on a tight schedule and has a lot to fit in. She appreciates quality and isn't afraid to splurge on it once in a while, as long as it's not an everyday thing. Sarah shops at Target.

Sarah shops at Oh My Cupcakes!

A lot of other people shop at Oh My Cupcakes!, too, but we sat down together one day as a staff and when we thought of the person who we see walk through the doors most often, we came up with Sarah. We named her Sarah because we feel like that's the name we see most often on her credit card, which usually has some fun picture on it and not just the boring old run of the mill bank logo. It might be a picture of her kids or a cute kitten or some pretty flowers but it's customized. Sarah's got attention to detail, and she appreciates it from us.

We can't please everyone so we do our best to target all that we do for Sarah. We know that time can be a precious commodity for her (oh sister, don't we know it) as she's rushing from one thing to the next, so we try to make her stop a quick and pleasant one. We know that sometimes she needs an extra smile or a cupcake of her own when she's picking up treats for the office, so we accommodate her in ways that make her feel special. Sometimes we even give her a mini for the road just because she was the good person who volunteered to go out of her way and pick up office treats. We hold the door for her when her arms are full of cupcake boxes and we remind her about online ordering so that even if it's 11 p.m. and she's loading the dishwasher when she remembers that she signed up to bring treats for the girls' class in the morning . . . we can come to her rescue.

We serve a variety of people each day, but when we tailor our services and decide what our guests would want . . . we try to think of Sarah. Sarah is our main audience.

When we choose how to spend our money on advertising, we think of where Sarah might be listening or watching or reading or hanging out. When we choose a new policy, we try to think if it will make life easier or harder for Sarah. Does it serve her, or us? If the answer is her, we're doing things right. If the answer is, "this really serves us," that's a big red flag, annoying buzzer, wrong answer. If a policy serves us instead of her, we need to go back and give things a second look.

If an advertising or partnership opportunity comes our way, we look at it through Sarah's eyes and decide if it will ever reach her or impact on her. If it's a no, then it's usually one of those opportunities we pass on, with a gracious, "This is a great opportunity for someone else, just not for us."

No, Sarah isn't our only guest, but she is representative for a lot of the guests that walk through our door. If we are making Sarah happy, hopefully we are making a lot of our guests happy right along with her. It's nothing new or revolutionary, lots of businesses do something similar, but this is how we do it.

A critical part of our cupcake journey has been keeping our audience or our primary guest in focus. It's tough when you are starting out and there are some great options coming your way. When there's someone sitting in front of you telling you, "This will be great exposure for your business, it's really a win-win." When faced with those difficult decisions, ask yourself, "does this even talk to the people I'm trying to talk to? Is this reaching my audience?"

Now that you know your audience, where are some places they're hanging out? For example, are they on Pinterest? What boards do they search? What magazines do they read? Where will you find them?

How will you best reach them?

What are your audience or primary customer's greatest needs?

What makes you the best person/company to address or care for those needs?

KNOW YOUR STRENGTHS

If there's one thing we seem to be amazingly gifted and talented at, it's discounting and reducing the gifts that God gave us. There's humble, and then there's just being stupid about it. Sometimes I'm stupid about it. I stick a magnifying glass on the things I can't accomplish and I minimize the things I do well. Are you ever stupid about it? Like when you get a compliment for something you're good at, and know you're good at it, then take that compliment and bat it aside?

"Wow that is an amazing portrait! I had no idea you were so good at watercolor!"

"Aw, thanks but I kind of messed up on her lips. See that big blob there? They turned out kind of weird."

You're nodding because you do this, right? I know, I do too. But why do we do this? That's not humility, that's stupidity. When we've got a strength, a gift, we need to use it, and not only use it, but be proud of it and let it shine. You are so beautiful, so talented and you are enough, sister. Give God a little credit for how awesome he made you. Truly, when you're batting those compliments aside, you're not giving God the credit for the gifts He's given you, and you're not giving yourself any credit for nurturing that strength or gift.

At Oh My Cupcakes!, we are good at cupcakes. Not pies. Not cinnamon rolls. Not cookies. Cupcakes. I've always wanted to be a cupcake shoppe. Will we ever branch out from that? Maybe . . . if those on our team have skills and strengths that grow beyond cupcakes. I know my own skills are not there, not right now. I never close doors, but I'm realistic about my own strengths.

The Balancing Act

What are the things you're good at? Come on, you can think of more than one or two. Whether I was good at them or not, I've thought of so many things I want to do in my life, I've really lost count of what they all were along the way. One of the things God gave me was an adventurous and curious spirit. I consider that a strength.

I was born to be a causer. I was born to be a "make it happen" girl. I've always thought I could do just about anything. I don't mean that to sound arrogant or cocky, I've just always been the type to look at something and think, "That looks like fun, I think I'll try it." It's how I got into radio, it's how I started a few businesses before Oh My Cupcakes!, and no doubt it's how I'll do a few more things in my lifetime.

Psalm 139:14

I praise you because I am fearfully and wonderfully made; your works are wonderful, I know that full well.

I'm an ideas girl and I like to see new things be born, new energy created, new life happen in the form of a business, a person's personal transformation, a promotion that came together or a new recipe that I've never tried before. I want to *cause* instead of *react*.

I think I was wired to make things happen, and when I'm not in that role, I'm discontent, restless, and angry. Anger turns to sadness, and soon I'm either getting my snark on, nit picking at people's shortcomings, or sulking and suddenly bursting into teary, shaking, violent crying fits in my office at 2 pm on a Thursday afternoon. (True story, you guys missed it but it was epic.)

I need to be *making*, and making something new. I'm a notorious starter, but not a grand maintainer. Oh, I can maintain for a while, but I need new challenge to feed my need to cause something new to exist in this world.

I've recently walked proudly into my forties, and in those years I have worked 26 different jobs. (Just recounted, it's 27). I graduated high school a semester early and was introduced to the 8-5 working world while everyone else my age was still walking the hallways between classes, going to prom, and celebrating Senior skip day. I wouldn't necessarily endorse early graduation with a thumbs up or a thumbs down vote, it was just the path I chose at the time.

I was no stranger to work though. During my 3 ½ high school years, I had been working as an evening janitor at an animal vaccine production facility from 4-8 pm every Monday-Friday. Not a lot of time for after school basketball games or other extracurricular activities, but I learned what it meant to have someone count on me to get a job done and learned if I didn't do a job right the first time, I'd have to do it again. And I definitely learned how to ride the buffer machine down the hallway without tipping it over or scuffing the wall. Talent.

After I left the hallways of West Lyon at semester time (insert obligatory Go Wildcats here) my first fulltime job was as a Guest Pay Reporting Coordinator at LodgeNet.

My Aunt Patty gave me $150 for a new professional wardrobe, and I spent that money with thought and care in every purchasing decision to stretch the budget. Growing up I had been clothed with gratitude and hand-me-downs courtesy of the racks of Goodwill and St. Vincent de Paul, so $150 was a fortune, and more than I had ever been allowed to spend on clothes in one shot. I felt so spoiled.

I was 17, out of school and dressed up like Barbie in my professional clothes, working as a Guest Pay Reporting Coordinator at LodgeNet. I had my own cubicle and a Macintosh 2E. Don't be jealous.

I had business cards, you guys . . .business cards with my name and title on them. I was so excited. I think I still have some floating around in the bottom of my hope chest, no joke. As a Guest Pay Reporting Coordinator, I was responsible for collecting data from hotel properties each morning on how many in-room movies were purchased the night before, if guests paid for them, and if there were problems *other than* maybe the guest thought the movie itself was crap. I used a fax machine and talked to people all over the country.

As a Guest Pay Reporting Coordinator, my first real professional 8-5 job, I experienced the taste of downsizing, company reorganization and layoffs firsthand just three short months into my position. So now, while everyone else my age was walking the hallways between classes, going to prom, and celebrating Senior skip day, I was being downsized from a company reorganization. I obviously hadn't experienced anything like that before and I thought my world was ending.

I did a short (and when I say short I mean two-weeks-short) stint in a textiles factory and learned that sewing the stitching across the bill of a baseball cap was not for me, nor was the assembly line life. I had to innovate or surely (after only two weeks I knew) I would suffocate and die.

Both the untimely layoff (has there ever been a timely one?) and the sewing factory job from hell really were catalysts to starting my first business. I started a home daycare which I ran totally like a preschool, back before I even had kids of my own. I look back on that home daycare and a couple of things come to mind:

1.) What on earth would possess me to think, at only 17-18 years old, that I could run an in-home daycare/preschool?

2.) Who would entrust a 17-18 year old who wasn't a mama herself to care for their kids all day every day?

Still, I was young enough and brave enough to just go for it, and my heart, confidence and determination were what made it work. I loved those kids like crazy and still remember so many of them, even twenty (plus) years later. My own little Bizzy Bee's daycare was really profitable and it was my first taste of running a business. I was hooked on what it felt like to be an entrepreneur.

Since the days of being a Guest Pay Reporting and a home daycare owner/operator, I've been (among many other things) a school bus driver dispatcher, a watch and jewelry repair person, a phone receptionist at a rape crisis center, a grocery store clerk, an independent Whole Life insurance sales associate, a bank teller and an on-air radio chick. I've started and owned a few small businesses along the way. I've tried a lot of things so far, because I want to experience everything life has to offer.

Many of my 27 jobs were simultaneous; I worked multiple jobs at a time because . . . well, finances. And because I like to try new things and I crave new challenge. Here's the realistic negative though--once the new and shiny of a job wears off and something starts to bore me, I'm *out*. I can't maintain. I realize that wasn't super responsible.

A Different Tune . . . Balance

Once I got into radio though, things changed. Each day was a whole new discovery with different music, different news, and different interactions with listeners. The challenge was always there because I wanted to create a better show every day. Radio held my attention far longer. Each day held its own new challenges and nuances and my soul was more fulfilled.

Life has its way of ebbing and flowing, of giving you the lessons you need at the time and taking away the things that no longer serve you. As I've been a business owner, I've discovered things have changed once again. Job-hopping isn't an easy option any longer. Now when the new-and-shiny of something wears off, I can't go find something different quite as easily as I used to. I find that when I maintain something for too long and I'm discontent, I disguise that discomfort with hard work, determined not only to work as hard as the next guy, but harder.

"Of course I should work six days a week," I tell myself, "I'm the owner, that's just what owners do."

My hard work might not look as traditional as hours you can count on a clock (because some weeks I'm not in the store clocking as many hours as the rest of the Cupcake Ninjas), it might just look like a lot of spinning thoughts I can't control and can't seem to get on top of. It's then I realize that I've taken the control out of God's hands and tried to take things over on my own. I lose sleep. I talk and think about work constantly. And I start to use that word much more often than usual: *work*.

See, over the journey this business has rarely felt like work to me because even when it's been hard, it's still been my dream. But when I'm in this mode of frustration and discontent and just . . . fighting with it all . . . it starts to feel a lot like work. I start to pick at and amplify the few wrong things instead of celebrating the many things that are right.

I do this teeter-totter thing: my rational mind takes over and I realize I don't need to work myself to death, so I step back a bit. Teeter-totter up. I try to slow my mind and body down so I can spend a few extra years on this earth and enjoy it, but then I feel like I'm not pulling my weight. Guilt sets in and begins to weigh; teeter-totter starts back down.

People don't see the work I do at home or understand the time I spend in my head, so the critical voice in the back of my head starts to whisper little lies: *everyone here thinks you're slacking ya know. They don't think you work as hard as everyone else on the team.* Teeter-totter crashes hard, the cycle begins again. You guys, it's ridiculous. I lose balance.

Comparison is the thief of joy

THEODORE ROOSEVELT

I will beat my body up, (who needs a sick day, right?) because I can convince my brain that if I'm working hard, I'm still making, creating, causing. I'll overbook my schedule, take on too many commitments, and work into exhaustion, only to realize that I've not *made* anything new, I've just been *reacting* to things going on around me. Soon my heart catches up and I'm still discontented and now heartsick because I realize I've been beating myself up over a cause that wasn't even mine. It's a dangerous lie that many dreamers and doers and entrepreneurs and business owners tell themselves: I constantly need to be working and doing.

Doing does not equal *creating*.

When I get into this mode, I also find myself comparing. Comparing myself to others, comparing my progress to another's progress, and comparing my success to another's success.

"Comparison is the thief of joy"
Theodore Roosevelt

Comparison is not only the thief of joy, it is also the language of the small. When I'm comparing myself to someone else's anything, I'm not focusing on my own journey, I'm focused on theirs. I'm not focusing on my own strengths, I'm focusing on theirs. I'm not focusing on the gifts I've been given, but theirs. And I'm comparing my struggles and my average to their highlight reel. It leaves me feeling petty and insecure. And definitely not within my strengths.

Creating is one of my strengths. I'm great at starting, visioning what can be, and beginning new things.

For instance, being in the office all day every day: not good for me. I thought for a while that I should be in there perched at a desk and solving problems. That makes sense, right? But I was finding myself drained at the end of the day, creatively just . . . gray, and unfulfilled. Unhappy.

But what's this about, God? This is my dream! I love these people. I love being here. I love being about Oh My Cupcakes! I truly enjoy greeting our guests and spending time with them. So why do I feel like I feel?

There are things about business ownership that do not bring me joy.

When I'm in the office, I don't feel like I'm creating anything new, I feel like I'm only reacting to things going on. I'm reacting to staff overages or staff shortages or high customer demands or worry there will be a lack of customer demand. I'm working on managing timesheets and placing advertising and hiring and most of it just isn't stuff that brings me much excitement or joy. It feels, to me, like reacting. It feels like wheel-spinning. It feels like comparing.

Now you understand, right? None of these things are wheel-spinning or reacting or comparing at all. These are all really important tasks that need to be done with care and excellence and dedication and prayer and love, like so many other things we do each day. But they are outside of the scope of my strengths. As we grew it was time for me to step out of the office and find an Operations Manager.

Amanda is our Operations Manager, and she is skilled at solving problems and creating processes. She's so happy to do these things, it is her joy. Critical thinking and problem solving are her strengths. They are her passion and make her feel fulfilled. She often says, "I just like seeing things work right. I like helping people find solutions." Me? I don't want to run things or oversee people or manage day to day operations. I don't want to figure out cost analysis comparisons, (bo-ring!) or do accounts payables, but these things are within the scope of Amanda's strengths and skillset.

Here's a hint: When you're working within the scope of your strengths and your best set of skills, you will also usually be the person who can do a task in a fraction of the time it takes someone, and you'll feel full of energy after working a long day at whatever you've been doing rather than feeling drained. That's what it feels like to be in balance with your strengths. It feels pretty amazing.

Only my kids and I have been on this Oh My Cupcakes! journey for it's entirety. My role has changed over the course of time. At this stage of business, the things that bring me the most joy are empowering and encouraging others in their roles and helping brainstorm events or working in new product development. I'm learning to embrace the changing role. Your role may change over time.

Identify which things you enjoy the most about what you do, so you can be prepared to adapt and embrace change as it comes your way as well. Why am I sharing all of this in a chapter called *Know Your Strengths*? Because the sooner you can identify and work within your strengths and spend your energy there, the sooner you can get rid of the things that drain you.

It's been a painful cycle for me, this teeter-totter of overworking and comparison-slinging. It's caused a lot of age (hello, wrinkle cream) heartache and tears. It's made me feel less "together" than at nearly any other time in my life. I've had so many "*what-the-heck-is-wrong-with-me-I'm-losing-my- mind*" moments I've lost count. I'm being transparent in showing you what it's been like for me because I want you to see that it doesn't have to be this way. Maybe I'm giving you a glance down your future road so you can heed it as a warning or an encouragement or just a word to the wise. I still haven't perfected this art of working within my strengths (and I do believe it's an art), but I'm getting better at it. I'm getting better at balancing the teeter-totter. And I've learned that when I'm working within my best strengths, the overworking and comparing really does fall away and I fight less battles within my own mind and heart.

Identify your strengths and surround yourself with people whose strengths shine in areas you aren't so gifted. In the beginning, the reality is you're probably going to be the one who does it all. I get that. But we're looking way off into the distance, remember? Not just six months down the road. As your dream grows, you have to be willing to admit which things you're not so great at, and hand them off to someone else.

Hey Lance. . . You Free?

If you're thinking *"Whoa, whoa, let's not get ahead of ourselves, there is no 'someone else,' it's just me here . . . and I won't be able to hire an employee for a while yet,"* hang tight. Look for people who do freelance work, they will be your best friends on your journey ahead. I had people who freelanced my accounting, my graphic design, and my website. They were invaluable partners in the growth process, and I wouldn't be where I am today without them! (Hi Madra, Lauren, Brady and Jaimen!) Freelancers rock. You need them and they need you, so you if you find the right people you can make some great partnerships. Also don't be afraid to keep an eye out for those people who cross your path that might make a great "X" one day, even if today isn't that day. Keep future-focused and when you're ready to hire your outstanding employees, you'll already have them in mind. They will be your best friends in helping you keep balance and work within your strengths, while letting them utilize their best strengths at the same time.

Doing the Hand-Off

Delegation was kind of challenging for me at first because well . . . I really do think I can do it all. Delegating things was also tough for me because I never want people to think that I'm asking them to do something that I'm unwilling to do. A good leader doesn't just delegate *the things they don't like to do* . . . they delegate *things they aren't good at*; they hand off the things people around them are gifted in, and everybody stays working within their strengths.

I still do dishes on a busy Saturday morning if it means it will best serve the team. I take the recycling out sometimes. There is nothing beneath me I've delegated, I've simply given away the things I'm not as *skilled* in. Big difference.

Now I know I've had 27 jobs so naturally you'd expect me to be good at everything, right? Totally kidding. I've discovered a lot of things I'm good at, and a lot of things I don't care ever to try again. But in working my strengths and admitting my boundaries, an interesting thing has happened. As I've handed things to people who are better than me, I've gotten the opportunity to watch them take us to newer heights.

Our kitchen Cupcake Ninjas, some of them trained pastry chefs, have bigger and better ideas than mine. They come up with amazing creations I couldn't imagine myself. Our fiscal bottom line has become less fuzzy and has morphed into something much clear and concise as our Accounting Ninja (not her official title, but it should be, right?) has put procedures and processes in place I never could have dreamt up myself. They've brought their strengths, their skills. And that's teamwork. You might not be there yet, to a point of delegating anything, but when you are, be sure you're confident enough in your own strengths and honest enough about your weaknesses to delegate things to others.

Today, my favorite role is to meet one-on-one with each person on staff and find out how their life is going inside and outside of the walls of Oh My Cupcakes! I have one or two time slots per week set aside for an off-site coffee or lunch where I can meet with people individually. I love finding out what each person's unique likes and passions are. I love asking what we can do better as a team and as a company, in their eyes. Today I'm sort of in charge of company culture and keeping people's hearts and minds engaged. I keep sharing the *original* vision of Oh My Cupcakes!, sharing everything we set out to be and ensuring we stay on that same path. If I keep breathing and sharing, it will help each person share it as well and we won't lose our original mission or vision even as we grow. Taking each person back to what we were at the beginning seems to be my best used strength and gift right now.

Now, some questions for you to reflect on your strengths:

Hey, what jobs have you had?
(Attach additional sheets as necessary.)

Take any external scenarios (like coworkers, schedules or bad bosses) out of the memory and think of the job only.

Which of the jobs were most fulfilling to you, and why?

_____

_____

_____

_____

Could these reflections help you decide or determine some of your future steps in building your idea?

_____

_____

_____

_____

What are your best strengths? Don't be shy about it, name them!

_____

_____

_____

_____

What's your typical reaction when someone tells you that you're good at something?

Confidence is a strength and a gift. Never underestimate its power in building your business. You can do this!

What should you say when someone tells you that you're good at something?

What things drain you or challenge you about building your business or idea?

Is there anyone you can hand them off to just yet?

KNOW YOUR BOUNDARIES

Like we discussed in the last chapter, Oh My Cupcakes! by virtue of the name alone, is pretty clear in what we do. We make cupcakes. We don't make pies. We don't make scones. Not cookies or those cute little cake pops. We make cupcakes. Cupcakes is what we do.

"Do you make cakes?"

Other than a few minor exceptions like the cutting cake for the top of a cupcake display . . . no. Cupcakes are our thing, and we stick to what we're good at. Again, I never want to shut doors so that may or may not change in the future if the skills of those on our team outgrow what we are doing right now, but I know what my personal strengths are. I've also learned about boundaries.

I remember back in the early days, a client asked me if we could do cupcakes for her daughter's birthday and then do one of those big cupcake cakes to go along with the order. I owned one of those big cupcake cake pans, but had never attempted baking one. I'd seen them done (super cute) and I loved how they looked in pictures, and I'm kind of the girl

who says, "Sure, let's give it a whirl, I think I can do that!"
So I told her exactly as much . . . I'd never actually done one,
but had the pan and so I was willing to give it a try.

The order was going to be done in two parts; vanilla almond
raspberry cupcakes on Friday night for the family party, the
big cupcake cake and another set of cupcakes on Saturday
morning for the kid party. Back then Brianna and I were still
renting space in our commercial kitchen, baking everything
there and delivering all orders direct to our customers.
Brianna and I would go in and bake in increments for each
order, decorate, clean up, and leave. Not terribly convenient
or efficient, but that's the way it worked at the time.

I was a little rushed on that Friday afternoon, as I had
packed a lot of things in. (Shocker). Brianna had no daycare
for her kids that afternoon and I was going solo but there
weren't too many orders that day so no big deal. Working in
the kitchen in solitude sometimes is a dance I really love. I
put the cupcake cake into the oven and baked it while I was
decorating the vanilla almond raspberry cupcakes for the
Friday portion of our client's order. I hummed along and did
my work in peaceful solitude, working through the rest of my
Friday orders while that big cupcake cake baked. My plan
was to come back to the kitchen and decorate the cake later
on that evening once it was cooled. I decorated the vanilla
almond raspberry cupcake order, and they were just lovely.

Man, that cupcake cake was taking a long time to bake.
I kept poking the tester into the middle, checking for
doneness and it just wasn't setting up. I waited around
for a while longer and then *finally* it was done all the way
through. I pulled it from the big convection oven but by this
time, I was really pushing up against my deadline for picking
Brandon up from school. My dilemma: wait and leave it in
the pan, or flip it out of the pan right now?

Here's what you need to know: One hundred out of one hundred times I'm the kind of girl to pick the, "*Go for it, do it now and let's just see how it turns out, what's the worst that can happen?*" method, rather than the one that will keep me waiting. Can you relate to this? I tell my kids all the time to put on their Patient Pants. . .but I definitely outgrew mine in about sixth grade.

The cupcake cake was warmer than I would have liked, but what the heck, I decided to de-pan it anyway. In one quick motion, I flipped the pan upside down so the cake would pop out in its two lovely pieces: bottom and swirly cupcake top. But instead of popping out of the pan in two pillowy soft, perfectly baked pieces like it was supposed to . . . the cake ripped apart, each side breaking in big chunks. Half of it stayed in the pan. Half of it came apart in crumbly pieces on my parchment-lined baking sheet. It was literally a hot mess. I had in front of me a steaming, crumbly vanilla bean disaster.

I thought quickly. Ok . . . plan B. I would go pick Brandon up from school, then bake another cake at home in my own oven, so the cake would be cooled and I could decorate it in the morning. I'd have to get up early on Saturday, but the rest of her Saturday order was already done so this was totally doable, no problem. No. Problemo. Easy peasy. Positive self-talk, folks, positive self-talk.

I grabbed the ingredients, pan and utensils I would need to bake from home. It was nontraditional, but hey . . . in a pinch you do what you do, right? I packed everything into my trusty little white Pacifica, including the cupcakes for her Friday evening order.

On my way to pick Brandon up from school, I called my customer to make Friday evening delivery arrangements.

"Ok, so I've got the vanilla almond raspberry cupcakes done for tonight's party. The big cupcake cake didn't turn out so well on my first attempt, so I'm going to bake another one tonight and will finish decorating it in the morning and then drop that by tomorrow with the rest of the cupcakes."

Silence on the other end of the line.

"Well," she hesitated, "the cupcake cake is for tonight's party, for pictures."

Ummmmm.

Now I'm a Plan B sort of girl, but this? Holy Plan B, C and D . . . I was not prepared for this. I don't know how I mixed up the signals, how we miscommunicated, how I misunderstood that the cake was for Saturday and not Friday, but holy crap, I was panicking. How could I mess this up so royally?

Again, I thought as quickly as I could. There had to be a solution.

"Ok," I said lightly, careful not to let my tone of voice betray the super outrageously freakalicious panic bubbling just beneath the surface. "What time is the party?"

"Well, it starts at 6 . . ." she trailed off. "But we wanted the cupcake cake for pictures we're going to do a little later, so the time really can be flexible." She was being so patient with me, so kind.

Since I had been honest with her about the cake "not coming out so well" that afternoon (which may have been the understatement of the year), she knew I would need to bake another one. I made arrangements to deliver her cupcakes prior to the party that evening and told her I would do the best I could with the delivery time of the cupcake cake. I said that it wouldn't make it by the party's six o'clock start time, but I'd have it there as quickly as I could. She was understanding.

I raced through the pickup lane at Brandon's school and squealed home. I put the cupcake cake into the oven and baked it. It baked and baked, once again taking forever. If I thought it took a long time in the commercial oven at the bakery, it took twice as long in my oven at home.

I had been texting all of the drama to Brianna, and she texted back a message that said she could help when Jared got home from work. Their whole family arrived and she tossed her coat quickly onto a chair as she passed through the living room. She washed her hands and rolled up her sleeves, assessing the status of our critical ~~patient~~ cake. It felt like any moment, nurses could come bursting out of adjoining rooms and update us on the cake's vitals, handing us scalpels all ER style. It was tense, folks. When the cake came out of the oven we tossed it into the freezer pan and all, willing it to cool so we could get it out of the pan.

Time was crawling and yet the hands on the clock face spun with abandon as we knew the party time was getting closer. We pulled the cake from the freezer and de-panned it . . . very, very carefully.

Success! The cake came out in one piece. We threw it back into the freezer, waiting to be able to frost and decorate. I am telling you the heat from that cake radiated from its insides. The earth's molten core is nothing compared to the temp that was inside that cake.

Fingers drumming on countertops, opening the freezer and checking intermittently, heels tapping . . . nothing sped the cooling process but everything added to our anxiety.

Of course we tried to frost it before it was ready. The frosting melted off. We had to scrape the cake off, stick it back into the freezer, let it cool some more and then start over again. Our customer called once during that time, "just checking in on us . . .?" We assured her we were frosting as fast as we could and would be there shortly.

The face cream industry thanks me for that cake debacle; I aged ten years in two hours. Finally the cake was adorned with delicate little swirls of pink and orange. A few polka dots covered the fondant goofs we made across the bottom, but overall it was pretty great for a first attempt and for all the stress we had been under. We high-fived, I placed the cupcake cake onto Brianna's lap in the car and hopped into the driver's seat, racing to the delivery.

It was about 7:30 pm in the middle of a dark South Dakota winter. Brianna cradled the cupcake cake carefully on her lap, breakable and precious as a child. As I braked gingerly to a stop at an intersection, Brianna could see the cake illuminated beneath the streetlights. I'll never forget the way she softly, quietly said, "Oh no . . ."

"Oh no?" I asked, panic in my voice. "What's 'oh no?' What do you mean, 'oh no'?"

Pink and orange curlicues of frosting were melting off the top and sliding down the edge of the cupcake cake. Frosting dropping like flies. Heat was still coming out from the inside of the cake. I wanted to cry. I wanted to give up. I wanted to throw up. Surely this little girl's birthday party was going to be ruined, all because of us. But . . . we were on our way to this delivery and had to bring what we had. *Ya run what ya brung*, isn't that what they say? It felt like Biblical times; peasants offering up an unworthy gift for a king. (Not overdramatizing here, am I?)

As we followed the directions to the address and turned down the street, I threw up in my mouth a little. It was a gated community, like million dollar plus homes. The rooftops were so tall they towered beyond my vision in the dark. I finally found it; the one at the end of . . . Amazing Street. Oh. My. Gosh.

Our customer came outside and met us in the front yard. Tears pricked at the corners of my eyes.

"We're late . . ." I said weakly, trailing off. The lump in my throat was huge. There's little I hate worse than letting someone down, but this felt like epic failure of grandest proportions. I reached into the car and carefully took the cake box from Brianna. "It just didn't turn out." I said flatly. "I'm sorry. Of course I won't charge you." I had to look away, I was just embarrassed at how badly I had failed my customer.

In that moment she did me the greatest kindness anyone could have done. She looked me in the eyes and said, "You know, I asked you to do something you told me you'd never attempted before. You were up front with me about the fact that it was new to you, but you tried it anyway. Thanks for trying."

She smiled at me, took the cakebox from my hands and after some brief discussion about Saturday's order, she went inside.

Brianna and I drove out of that beautiful gated community, away from the gorgeous home at the end of Amazing Street, and I felt like a weight had lifted. It certainly wasn't because I felt better about things; I felt like I had failed and I was still beating myself up pretty badly. But I had been gifted with grace and kindness, and those two things makes all the difference in the world.

And that cursed cupcake cake was out of my hands and that felt pretty good, too.

Boundaries, Risk and Mediocrity

The author and marketing guru Roy H. Williams points out two truths on boundaries, risk, and mediocrity. The first is this: *"If you can't tell funny stories about embarrassing mistakes you've made, you're not taking enough chances."* Funny story and embarrassing mistake: CHECK!

The second piece of advice is, *"You learn a little from small mistakes. You learn a lot from big ones. You learn nothing at all from mediocrity. Failure is never a waste of time. Mediocrity always is. The fear of failure is what keeps you average. Success is the result of taking chances."*

Failure is never a waste of time, so remember to take chances and risk. You may read over the past couple of paragraphs and think, "Come on, you just told me this story about an epic failure like that one, and now you're encouraging me to risk boldly? Plus you're telling me to know my boundaries. Aren't those things opposites?" I don't necessarily think they are. I think there needs to exist a healthy amount of risk accompanied with a bit of prudence and knowledge of what is *realistic*.

I hadn't been realistic with myself about what a cupcake cake involved. Honestly, I didn't have enough information to even know the time or prep it involved. I hadn't ever greased and floured the pan or baked one in the oven up until that first time. But I risked, I failed and I learned. Thankfully, I was gifted with grace and kindness in the face of what I considered my failure. If you're starting a business, I imagine you've got some fears about risk, don't you? Risk is going to be involved, and sometimes you're going to fail. Sometimes you're going to fail epically. Sometimes you're going to find a win or an outcome that was different or better than you could have ever imagined.

Knowing Your Boundaries = Being Realistic

Being realistic is not my strong suit. I'm a dreamer and if you're an entrepreneur I'd venture to guess you have a dreamer's spirit, too. That's awesome. You've got to take chances and be willing to risk, but you've also got to be mature enough to know your own boundaries. When I was asked to make this first cupcake cake, there were some reasons I wasn't very realistic about things. Mainly, I hadn't yet learned how to say "no," because I desperately wanted to please everyone.

Being realistic means I know what I'm capable of and what I *want* to be capable of. I can't please everyone and neither can you. I can't say yes to everything and neither can you. I'm also not good at everything, and neither are you. And when you try to please everyone and do everything and be good at everything, sometimes you fail epically and pink and orange curlicues of frosting slide off the side of your cake. Knowing your boundaries sometimes simply means being realistic about your true capabilities.

On that next Saturday morning I delivered the rest of the cupcakes for the next party. My stomach churned once again as I drove down Amazing Street, and I tried not to relive all the failure from the night before. I tried to focus on all the good instead.

"How was the party?" I asked through a half-smile.

"The party was great," my client answered. "There was one side of the cake that was perfect for pictures. And the best part? We got to eat warm cake! It was delicious."

I had set out to be a gourmet cupcakery, offering the best cupcakes with the most amazing flavor around. Through that experience I learned cupcake cakes were outside the scope of my expertise. I had to learn my boundaries. Nearly as important as having a big and dreaming vision, you need to have a set of parameters around the things you can't do. The things you don't do. The things you won't do. You cannot please everyone. On a surface, logical level we all know this. But we need to get deeper and realize that fact on a heart level.

Any time you have either a failure or a success, it's so crucial to focus on the lessons you can take away from the situation. So, what did I learn? What would I have done differently? How would I have been more realistic about things?

1. I would have been a little better prepared. I would have tried to bake a "trial run" cupcake cake first, days before her order, so I knew if I was even capable of putting out a quality product for my customer.

2. I would have been more patient when depanning that first cake. (Life lesson there, kids.)

3. I would have allowed more margin and built in more time in case things went wrong.

Since that time, Oh My Cupcakes! has gained some amazingly talented people who have made the most beautiful and imaginative cupcake cakes for our customers; something I'm not skilled at doing. We rock at them now. We also know we have a limit to how many we can take on in a weekend to do them well. They take time. Even though we've expanded our offerings to include those gorgeous cupcake cakes now and we execute them marvelously, we know our boundaries and we're realistic about what we are capable of to best serve all of our guests.

Saying "no" isn't a defeat. Sometimes saying "no" is the best answer at the time, given your circumstances, so you can best serve all of your guests or customers.

Would you say you're a risk-taker or a play-it-safe'r"?

What risks have you taken thus far in your business venture?

What risks are you avoiding?

Have you found yourself pushing your boundaries?

Could this lead to a situation where you could possibly get into a situation of "overpromise and under-deliver" like I did with my cupcake cake customer?

Who are trusted "advisors" in your life who can keep you accountable to taking some healthy risks while keeping realistic about your own boundaries?

KNOW YOUR WIN

What does success look like to you? I've never defined success in the same ways others have defined it.

For a lot of companies (not all) they look at the bottom line to determine success. Is the company making money? Yay! Success. Is the company losing money? Boo. (Insert Debbie Downer noise.) Sad day.

Money isn't a win to me. Now, it would be silly to ignore money and ignore numbers. More than a little silly, it would be foolish. If we ignore numbers, we can't take care of the families who are impacted by the jobs created at Oh My Cupcakes!

I don't care for numbers as a rule but I do love storytelling and Amanda tells me *numbers tell a story.* We can learn a lot from the story those numbers tell. That being said, numbers are not our *primary* focus at Oh My Cupcakes!

In fact, I find that I can get distracted by numbers if I pay too close attention, so that's why our Operations Manager Amanda, is so awesome in her role. When I get too distracted by them, I take my focus off of our true goals and I start comparing stuff I have no business comparing. I start using the language of the small (see Know Your Strengths), and I forget to focus on our wins. I sort of forget what wins are even dressed like or how to pick them out of a crowd. When I get too focused on numbers, I get all short of breath and think I need to get my needy and nervous little hands on the controls of every detail (there's that teeter totter crashing down again) when you and I both know full well that God controls all of it. Chill, sister. Breathe it out. Relax. And this is why I don't pay such close attention to the money of it all.

You guys, it's so important to identify early on what you'll consider a point in the win column, and how you're going to define when and if you've scored. For your business, maybe it's something quantifiable like a certain number of caramels or dog treats produced in a period of time, a specific number of aprons stitched in a month or a certain number of new customer contacts each week. Maybe it's a specific number of new orders. But you've gotta know what your wins are, how they're dressed and how to pick them out of a crowd.

My wins have been things that are directly correlated with our values. We added new benefits last year like an IRA (which we match) and health insurance. We have kids as young as sixteen who are contributing to their retirement funds and we are matching their contributions. We're helping them plan for their futures. I get jazzed about that. That directly correlates with our value of *family* because those benefits enrich the families who work at Oh My Cupcakes! Throw a few points up in the win column. Yeah baby! When we are able to donate large amounts of money to an organization we're passionate about or serve in our community it correlates with our value of *generosity*. Winner, winner, chicken dinner.

Walt Disney said he wanted every guest to leave the Disney parks after a long day wearing the same smile they came in wearing; that was how he identified a win. (I also have a theory that when you inevitably see at least half the guests at any Disney park wearing mouse ears, that, my friends, is also a win.) At Oh My Cupcakes!, when a guest places a special order with us and they come to pick up that order, we want their face to show delight as they look into their box. We want their smile to show that *they notice* the special care we put into their order, and that they feel our attention to detail and our care because of it. That's a win to us.

I know those wins are somewhat intangible because you can't track them on paper, but I believe if you focus on making those intangible wins come alive, the numbers that so many people focus on will naturally follow. You don't become successful by reaching boldly for success; it's not one big movement. You become successful by making little choices and taking small actions each day that propel you closer to your wins. You'll reach your point of desired success only when you learn to identify those little things that add up to the big things. If you don't learn to pay attention to them and celebrate them along the way, it's going to be a pretty long and miserable journey.

What do you identify as a win?

_____

_____

_____

Has it changed since you've begun your journey?

_____

In what way do you think it will continue to evolve?

_____

_____

_____

_____

How can you celebrate those wins and call attention to them so that when your journey gets rough, you'll have a reminder of how far you've come?

_____

_____

_____

_____

Win or Lose . . . Sometimes It's Really Not Your Fault

I've read a pretty good amount of books on leadership and I'm always trying to learn more about how to be a better leader, how to create a better culture, how to breathe excellence into our workplace. I want us to be the best. Not for pats on the back or so we can be best _just for us_, we want to give our guests the best and give God the glory. We haven't created this by ourselves, although I give mad props and incredible gratitude to the team of Cupcake Ninjas who have baked a billion cupcakes and breathed our mission statement every day. God has created this and I want to be the best so people can see His goodness through us. I want to show the world what God can do with something as simple and small as a cupcake.

In any leadership book I've read though, I've never seen the chapter that talks about what happens when you do everything right and things go wrong anyway. When you have the most pure and true intentions and things fail. This might be down the road a little bit for you or maybe it's where you're at right now, but I want your heart to be prepared and I think it's so important for you to hear this.

What do you do when you give of your heart and you pray for your team and their families and you all serve your guests and the community together and then suddenly a key person comes into your office out of the clear blue sky and says they've taken another position away from your company and your dream? What then, Chicken Little?

Dear friend, I want to hold your heart so gently right now if you are going through this. It's such a painful time. Some of the most painful times I've endured in my time thus far have been the losses of staff at Oh My Cupcakes! It's a grieving process because it's the loss of a family member.

If you have no idea what I'm talking about, I hope you never come to this crossroads . . . but I'm pretty sure you will. I'm pretty sure everyone does at some point.

I want you to listen and remember this when you've reached that crossroads: I want you to realize that it's not your fault. After these years and some painful losses I've come to realize: everyone has their own universe, and it spins outside of ours at Oh My Cupcakes! Everyone has their own set of outside circumstances and situations that are 100% unaffected by what they do in the workplace and who they are within our walls. Those situations and circumstances are 100% more important in their lives than anything they do at Oh My Cupcakes!

Your business is *your dream*, not theirs. They may be firmly and wholeheartedly dedicated to you and your business, but their earth revolves around a different sun than your earth does. And to their universe, they're *committed*. If their earth is off its axis for whatever reason, they're going to do whatever they think they need to do to right its position once again. If their earth has a shot at a better universe, they're going to do whatever they can do to make their universe better.

You would do the same thing if you put yourself in their position. I would, too. It might be impossible to understand as you're blinded with your tears of loss when your key staff, family member, teammate is telling you they're leaving . . . but you see it in your heart, you do. That's maybe why it hurts so much.

Leaving your company might be the hardest thing they've ever had to do, but they're leaving anyway. My friend, you can't take it personally. You must realize that in some circumstances, no matter how hard you try to be a good leader, it simply has *nothing to do with you*. When you're a family, losing a family member hurts.

When you know what your win is, you will be better equipped to handle turnover and situations like that. You'll look at things objectively (after you've cried your tears and eaten a bag of Sea Salt and Cracked Pepper kettle chips. And some ice cream. And some chocolate.) You'll realize that they're doing what they think is best for their family and if you're going to stay committed to your values, you need to support their decisions.

You'll know that, even if it hurts right now, if you're focusing the important things like your mission statement and your wins, you can keep going for another day.

Have you experienced a loss yet?

_____

How did focusing on your wins help you get through it?

_____

_____

_____

_____

KNOW YOUR SELF

I used my voice in radio to entertain people, to get important information across when severe weather was nearby and to tell people what was going on with their favorite musical artists. I've got a voice that has told my kids just how much I love them and has tried to be encouraging to people around me. I don't always get it right, but I've tried to use my voice to be kind. The voice I use on the outside sounds a lot different than the one I use on the inside. The voice I use on the inside sometimes takes a different tone with me than it takes with other people.

Do you have that inside voice? It's the questioning voice, the skeptical voice, the critical voice. The voice that asks, "Who do you think *you are* to try this, anyway? How dare you dream so big? Why do you even bother?" That voice won't leave me alone sometimes.

That voice isn't good to me. It doesn't speak to me with love and care and encouragement like it speaks to everyone else. I've got to shut that voice up, and you do, too. I was the one to jump in the driver's seat and push on the gas to create Oh My Cupcakes!, and *you* are the one to do the same thing to build your dream. You are the most uniquely qualified and well-equipped because this is your big dream. Keep moving it forward.

You know that inner voice that doesn't speak with care and love? It lies. Tell it to be gentle, tell it to be kind. Use storytelling to tell that voice to be quiet. Tell yourself a different story, and keep doing what you know you need to do to move forward.

Commit to doing one thing every day to bring you closer to your dream. Whether it's a little thing or a big thing, I did something each day that kept me moving from our small rented kitchen to the Oh My Cupcakes! we have today. I know myself, and I know if I get off track even for a little while, I'll lose my momentum. (Hello, Facebook? Pinterest? These can derail my momentum for hours/days/weeks.)

Knowing myself and being honest with myself about my own struggles has been key to getting us from there to here. Be honest with yourself and pay attention to the things that keep you focused and the things that get you off track. Make adjustments accordingly.

What lies does that inner voice tell you?

How can you silence that voice and speak to yourself with kindness and love and tell yourself a different story?

_____

_____

_____

_____

What leads you closer to your dream?

_____

_____

_____

What pitfalls lead you off-track?

_____

_____

_____

_____

Let's put some protections and accountability in place.

When I find myself getting off track, I will bring myself back by:

Lead With My What?

Owning this business has brought me the most soaring feelings of joy, the highest feelings of success, and also the most crushing lows, feelings of failure, mourning and loss I think I've ever experienced. These extreme highs and lows both stem from the same place: *the deepest reaches of my heart.* If I didn't care so much, I wouldn't be able to embrace the feelings of joy and euphoria I'm able to feel when we experience a win as a team. If I didn't care so much, I wouldn't feel such real pain when we have a moment of failure and let a customer down or take it so personally when someone on our team decides to move on by either moving across the country or finding another job-home.

I do everything in this business with my whole heart. And even though it opens me up to a lot of vulnerable squishy feelings of joy and hurt, I wouldn't and shouldn't do it any other way. My team knows exactly who I am because I'm authentic with them. They get *me*, for better or for worse. For stupid dance moves and belting lyrics on a Saturday morning (you oughta hear my version of "Gimme One Reason" by

Tracy Chapman) or for tears in my office on a Tuesday, they get *Melissa*. Everybody here is on this journey with me and I try my best not to hide from them. Even when it's messy and hard and I wonder what they're thinking of me or if I'm being an "ok" leader. I trust in the relationship we've built thus far. It's my hope that they can trust in me even more for showing them all I go through as an owner and person; both good and bad. Lead with your heart. Lead with your whole, messy and beautiful heart.

Make Up Your Mind

I'm a positive person. It's not always easy, but it's generally my persona. Abraham Lincoln said, "People are about as happy as they make up their minds to be." I do believe it's a choice and I choose most days to be generally happy. Make up your mind to be happy. No, it's not always easy. I've found it especially hard in business when I've had weeks (they're a part of any business, I'm afraid) when I've felt like I've just been kicked down and I haven't felt much like being the cheerleader anymore. I've felt like I'm a poor leader. I've had my confidence shaken. I've had weeks where the tears have been a daily occurrence and my smile has been a little pasted on through the anxiety I'm feeling on the inside.

But through it I've been able to step back and say, "Ok God, what's next? What is the lesson you want me to learn from this? What's the next right thing and how can I set about to doing it?"

Weeks like that, it's more important than ever to make up your mind to go to bed and rest, then get up tomorrow and start over. You've got to know yourself and know *what* you are about at the core of you, so you don't forget *why* you're here, doing what you're doing. I'm about the values I named in an earlier chapter. I'm about family, faith and generosity.

LEAD WITH YOUR WHOLE MESSY & BEAUTIFUL HEART.

I'm about being a professional encourager. In the end I don't really make cupcakes because I like to bake or because I enjoy sweets (although, come on, they're a pretty great perk), I have this business because of what I want to be about.

Be Defined by Who You Are, Not What You Do

Here's what I want you to know. I want you to promise me you won't let success or failure define you. Neither of them *are* you, so neither of them should define you. Go to bed at night and rest in knowing that you've done the best you can with what you have, and let the rest of it go.

I confess to you in full disclosure that even as I'm writing this, this week has been one of *those* weeks. A week where I've felt a little like the punches and hits keep coming, and I'm fretting over an order that didn't go as planned and a situation that was out of our control. I'm trying like mad to let it go but it's not easy. I've had losses and sorrows this week and I'm wondering why God has me writing this chapter right now. Like, really, God? But I think it might be because I needed to take a little dose of my own advice.

As your business grows, everyone will think they know you. You'll begin to be associated with and recognized because of your business.

"Hey, you're the Cupcake Lady, right?"

"Hey, aren't you the guy who has the DJ company?"

"You're the lady who makes the designer bags. I know you."

I know you. People think *they* know you, so *you* better know you. *You* are not *your business* or *company*, you are an intricate design of ideas and hopes and insecurities and flaws, stitched together delicately with your experiences and dreams and values. You better know you inside and out, because no one else's head is hitting your pillow at night. There will be the unsolicited advice that comes your way, so be ready for it. There will be the, "you-can't-do-it's" and the "gee, did you ever think about's" and the behind-your-back-talkers along your journey. Be strong enough to know who *you are* so you can ignore them.

Sometimes you'll encounter people who will try to prevent you from becoming what you were purposed to be. Be wise enough to recognize them and bold enough to walk away if it's what will protect your heart and your dream and your purpose. But also? Be humble enough to listen in case they have something to offer that you really haven't thought of. Listen objectively and then trust your gut.

Starting a business will change you in ways you never imagined. That's easy to type and even easier to read and skip right over, but go back and take that in; absorb it. Feel it deep within your being and do the best you can to understand it from where you're sitting today.

Starting and owning a business will change you in ways you never imagined, both good and bad. Do it anyway. Go for it anyway.

Don't Forget to Have a Little Fun

Sometimes I get to feeling like the line from that CSNY song Judy Blue Eyes that says, "It's getting to the point where I'm no fun anymore." Or maybe you identify with The Joker from the Batman movies: "Why so serious?"

Owning a business can be serious . . . well . . . business. As we've grown, more responsibilities have been added to our plate. More clients have come to trust in us to take care of their events or to carry out their special moments. We don't take that lightly and we don't want to let them down. More employees have come to rely on Oh My Cupcakes! for their income and for their livelihood. It can be a weighty position, taking care of so many people. When you lead with your whole heart, it can be soul-demanding work. But don't forget to take care of yourself, and don't forget to have a little fun.

I have a very wise friend named Travis. I called Travis one morning and asked him what he was working on for the week. He's usually pretty driven and motivated and task-focused like I can be, so his answer surprised me. He said, "I'm working on walking slow."

Don't become so driven that you forget to walk slow. Take days off. Enjoy the sunshine and when you're in it, really experience it. Walk slow.

Who am I? Who am I really? Write a few words that define who you are, *not related* to your business or dreams.

What will happen to you if you succeed wildly at this dream or idea?

What will happen if your dreams don't go as you've planned and they fail in what might be a traditional sense of failure?

Who matters most in your life?

What will their opinion be if you either succeed or fail?

_____

_____

_____

_____

"The most important work you and I will ever do will be within the walls of our own homes."
Harold B. Lee

What do you like to do to have fun?

_____

_____

_____

_____

When can you schedule in some fun time?

_____

_____

We schedule appointments and meetings and doctor visits and things that fill up our calendar. Schedule in time for fun. Schedule it out at regular intervals, six months ahead if you need to, but don't cancel out on those appointments any more than you would cancel out on a doctor visit. Stay committed to having fun. Please trust me on this one.

KNOW YOUR GOD

It doesn't make sense, how we got from there to here.
When our store was downtown for three and a half years
we closed at 2 pm every day. We've always been closed on
Sundays. Our business model probably doesn't make sense
on paper. How in the world did we make the journey from
renting space in a sketchy commercial kitchen to having two
beautiful locations and shipping nationwide? I don't honestly
know. How did we do it all without incurring debt? One
simple step and small act of faith at a time. One tiny gulp
and tiny risk at a time. I see God's hands in every step of the
way from beginning chapters to now. God did this.

Please don't think it's been easy. If you only knew. Oh you
guys, if you only could see how many times I've sat in my
office, shaking and sobbing and in tears thinking, "there's no
way we can overcome this. There's no way to get out of this
one." I think, "I've failed."

We've been given challenge among the sweetness.

But every time we get the opportunity for a new day. We
come into the quiet kitchen early the next morning before
the sun is awake and flip the switches on the ovens to "on"

once again. We scoop some flour and sugar out of the bins, crack and whisk some eggs, start measuring ingredients and making batter, and we stay focused on what we know we're about: shining God's love and making people smile with cupcakes. We unlock the doors at open and people come in to buy cupcakes. We do our best to make them feel like a guest being warmly welcomed into our home. Once again, we have been blessed with another day and the opportunity to share joy and a special moment with them.

We get through the challenging times by knowing who our God is and by moving ever forward. I think we learn the most about our team, about ourselves and about one another in the challenging times. We learn most about what we are made of, and we learn how strong our faith really is.

We were founded on Proverbs 16:3—*"Commit your work to the Lord and your plans will succeed."* In the beginning that verse was scrawled on a piece of notebook paper with red marker and hung on a wall in the commercial kitchen. Now it's in gorgeous calligraphy on my office wall. It's kind of a metaphor for how far we've come; from a humble beginning to a beautiful now. God has taken something so simple . . . a delicate little handmade confection, and He's turned it into something much bigger. We've always tried to stay focused on Him. We don't always get it right and many times we need to readjust our focus. We're human and our vision gets skewed.

But I could tell you story after story of times when God has worked the coolest things through what we do each day. He's brought people into Oh My Cupcakes!, either guests or employees, that became deep relationships about so much more than cupcakes. I have friends in Texas, Arizona, Oregon, Uganda, Oklahoma, and California because of this place. I have a foster daughter who comes in and out of my life because of a work relationship that began here.

I get to be part of her life because of this. I'm in tears as I write these words and think about all the people who have come through the doors of Oh My Cupcakes! and the grand plans God had all along. When I was dreaming, I never could have dreamt this big. His plans were and continue to be so much bigger than mine.

And that's why it's so important that you grab hold of your big dream and you go for it. If you're feeling it purposed in your heart, you are meant to pursue it. Fears may want to hold you back, but God does not write fear. God writes faith. God says, "*Stick with me, kid, we got this, but buckle up because it's going to be a crazy journey ahead.*"

My hope is that as long as we keep moving forward at Oh My Cupcakes!, we will continue to succeed and grow and make an impact in our community and with one another. I want to continue to take big risks that don't make sense on paper when my gut says it's right, because that's what faith is all about.

I don't know what God looks like to you, but to me God looks like a journey that has taken us down a path from $67 and a big dream to a point where we can now help support families. To a place where we can make a big difference for people around us. Where we can create smiles and spread joy. To me that's pretty cool. Thanks, God. Thanks for the messy parts and the hurts, thanks for the times I've doubted myself and had nothing to rely on but you. Thanks for the hard work and the easy days. Thanks for the silliness and the joys. Thanks for the times when we get to be part of people's special moments. I hope I never take any of it for granted, not one second. Thanks God, for it all.

April 8, 2015 Sioux Falls, SD

WITH BLESSINGS
AND GRATITUDE

A lifetime is a journey, and one not to be taken lightly. As you and I embark on our separate excursions, each of us treading lightly on our own terrain, it is a miracle when our paths cross ever so gently without bumping into one another and causing harm. I've been so fortunate, so highly favored to have encountered some beautiful warriors which have made life richer and made me more appreciative for all the beauty that exists on the well-worn trail and off.

Randi, Emily and Brandon, you are the reason I do what I do. You can be *anything* . . . go do it and go be it. Fly. Little Lyric Rose, I don't know what the future holds but I know I love you to the top of the house and the top of the sky, and that's enough for today. Mom and Dad, you are the first beautiful warriors I ever knew. So many gifts you've given me like the gifts of resilience and work ethic and that "damned old positive attitude." I wouldn't be who I am without you. Amanda, you're my best friend. You're the one who keeps it all together, keeps me sane and keeps my ideas at least partially grounded in reality. I'm so grateful.

Trav, buddy I'm honored to be in your circle. Thanks for knowing my crazy and loving me anyway. Travel well. C.W., thank you for being my friend when we were married and staying my friend now that we're not. You're a good man, an amazing father, and I wish you happiness and all good things. Jodi, you gave me encouragement and asked me hard questions when I needed both of those things. Thank you for buying me the first roll of 100 decorating bags so I could stop washing out the same 10 and reusing them over and over.

To every Cupcake Ninja who has ever learned to say "my pleasure" or woken at 3 am to come join our crazy team, I'm grateful for the time you spent with us. Whether your season was long or short, you've left your mark and I'm thankful for the time we had together. For the Cupcake Ninjas at Oh My Cupcakes! *right now*, thank you for allowing me the time to write this book. I hope I've honored you and done well by you. Our team is the strongest and most beautiful it's ever been and I love working with you every day.

So many mentors and friends have altered my trajectory: Sheri, you are my business rock star. Lauren, seriously… your talent and passion are outstanding. Mrs. Ractliffe, thank you for first believing in me. Jon Gordon, thank you for the opportunities. I'm still amazed I *get to* work with you. Brooke, you are the rock star of all rock stars and I don't know how you keep it all together. Breathe, smile, and relax, you deserve it. My dear friend Bob, our chance meeting in the Jacksonville airport on your 80th birthday has forever enriched my life. Carrie, I know why I went to Haiti, it was to deepen my friendship with you. I love you and your family. Jolene, you're a mighty warrior. Sarah W., you are doing big things, the world better watch out for what's yet to come. Wynne, thanks for praying. Colby Family, your role in all of Oh My Cupcakes! cannot be quantified; it's too grand. Trish Dougherty, Carolyn Thompson, Jake, Lisa Uhlir, you can't know how much I look up to you. Mariah, I'm inspired by how you seek God before anything else. Keep seeking. Ben and Patty, you guys always believed in me. Dan from Simon's Catering…thank you for my first "break." Ryan; has anyone ever thanked you for not giving them money? Thank you for the best "not exactly yes" I've ever gotten. And of course, my rock star Starbucks crew. Couldn't have written this without the toffee nut latte love from you. Chef Amy, you are one of my original rock stars and I'm still in awe of you.

Countless friends from radio, friends from church, and friends I've met on the street, in grocery store checkout lines and in coffee shops have made my life more beautiful. You have created Oh My Cupcakes!

I have been given countless opportunities and am grateful for every single one. I owe so much to so many...but most of all, I owe it all to God for laying out this grand path itself. I pray that I would continue to walk steps of integrity and honor God in all I do.

ABOUT THE AUTHOR

Melissa Johnson is a writer who travels and a traveler who writes. Melissa is a mother of three, a business owner and an eternal optimist. She speaks to school districts, corporations, non-profits and civic organizations about living life with passion and purpose. Her background lies in media and communications and she has delivered keynotes and workshops for the Jon Gordon Companies for over 6 years. She considers determination, a relentless desire to serve others, and unshakable optimism among her greatest gifts. She lives in Sioux Falls, SD with her children, her faithful dog Sasha, and her cat Nigel, who is a loveable jerk.

> *"I simply want to leave this world a better place than it was when I got here. I have a lot of work to do before I go."*

Websites

melissajcreative.com
ohmycupcakes.com

Blog

believethebestinothers.com